TINY TALKS

I AM A CHILD OF GOD

HEIDI DOXEY

CFI, an imprint of Cedar Fort Publishing,
Springville, Utah

Dedicated to Samantha JoAnn,
my middle-name twin

ISBN 13: 978-1-4621-2095-6

Published by CFI, an imprint of Cedar Fort, Inc., 2373 W. 700 S., Springville, UT 84663
Distributed by Cedar Fort, Inc., www.cedarfort.com

LIBRARY OF CONGRESS CATALOGING-IN-PUBLICATION DATA ON FILE

Cover design by Shawnda T. Craig
Cover design © 2017 by Cedar Fort, Inc.
Edited and typeset by Chelsea Holdaway

Printed in the United States of America

10 9 8 7 6 5 4 3 2 1

Printed on acid-free paper

Contents

Introduction

We are so blessed to know that we are children of a loving Heavenly Father who cares about each one of us and wants to help us become better. This knowledge blesses us each day with an ability to clearly see what our role is in this life and how we can help others learn their value as well. We are not simply ordinary people without purpose or direction. Our lives have meaning because we are children of God with divine potential.

Children often have an innate sense of their divine worth. Children who have grown up in happy, loving families know what it feels like to be loved unconditionally. They can feel Heavenly Father's love in the love that they receive from their parents, grandparents, and other family members. We can help them to better understand what their loving relationship with Heavenly Father means for their lives now and in the future.

This year in Primary, we are focusing on the sacred relationship that we each have with our Father in Heaven. I hope that as you teach the children you love about their Heavenly Father and His love for them, you will feel His love for you also. We all have things that we can improve upon, but our Heavenly Father's love for us never wavers. He is always ready to forgive us of our mistakes and guide us to become better.

I know that Heavenly Father will also allow you to feel the love He has for each child that you teach. They are precious to Him. As you serve them, you will be able to glimpse their divine potential as spirit children of our Heavenly Father. Share these feelings with the children as you are prompted to do so by the Spirit.

I am grateful for loving parents and teachers who helped me to discover and cherish my divine worth as a daughter of God. I know that He loves all of us, cares about our lives, and has a plan for each of us. I hope you will use this year in Primary as an opportunity to strengthen your own relationship with our Heavenly Father and encourage the children you love and teach to do the same.

HOW TO USE THIS BOOK

This book is designed to help you prepare for Primary with ideas for lessons, talks, scriptures, songs, and more. For each chapter, you will find an overview of resources that can be used throughout the month. Next, you will find specific ideas for each week of the month, including talks and scriptures your children can give in Primary. Each week also includes a lesson and activity specifically written to be used in sharing time. With a little adaptation, these lessons and activities can also be used in your home for family night or family scripture study, or as part of a lesson in a Primary class.

The last section of the book focuses on ideas and tips for the annual Primary presentation, with suggestions for learning the specific songs and a sample presentation outline.

MONTHLY OVERVIEW

Multimedia Resources

In recent years, the Church has created a wonderful library of videos and other interactive materials that can be accessed online. For each month, you'll find a suggested list of multimedia resources or online videos (with links) that you can use at any point throughout the month. Sometimes we learn best by having materials presented to us visually, so these videos can be a great way to engage children who might otherwise have a hard time paying attention. Before using one of these videos in Primary, be sure to download it to your device or check to make sure you can stream it quickly at the church.

Songs

The songs listed at the beginning of the month will help you prepare for your annual Primary presentation. Any time you see a bolded song title, that is one of the songs that is specifically meant to be included in your Primary presentation. By focusing on one or two of these songs each month, you won't have to learn all new material right before you give the presentation. In addition to these songs, you'll also find some other songs listed that fit in with the theme for that month, as well as a few classic favorites that can be used all year long. Unless otherwise specified, all songs are from the *Children's Songbook*.

Gospel Art Book

Each month includes a suggested picture from the *Gospel Art Book* that can be displayed in your home or Primary room. You can refer to this picture throughout the month as a visual reminder to the children of that month's specific theme. Changing the picture monthly will help to keep these themes fresh in the children's minds.

WEEKLY SECTIONS

Scripture

The weekly scripture reference is meant to help you find scriptures for a child to give as part of your opening exercises. You may also want to encourage children to share an article of faith in addition to the scripture for the week.

Talk

Each week includes a sample talk that would be appropriate for a child to give in Primary. The stories in these talks can also be used during the lesson or in family home evening or in another setting. While the stories and language are intended to be simple, the concepts and doctrines they illustrate are profound. To foster understanding, you may want to have the child giving the talk illustrate a few of the main ideas visually, or share how this story relates to their own life. At the end of the talk, have the child bear a brief testimony.

Lesson

The lessons included with each week are to help leaders, teachers, and parents prepare for a sharing time, class lesson, or family home evening. The basic structure of the lessons is to begin with a discussion, followed by an activity and an application and review. You may wish to use only part of the lesson or modify it to fit the needs of your children. The Spirit will help you to know how best to teach the principles you want to convey.

The lessons have been designed to involve minimal preparation and planning. While they may include some movement or active participation by the children, they are also meant to be reverent enough to be done in a church building on Sunday. At times, you may need to remind the children that they are in a house of the Lord and that their voices, behavior, and tone should always reflect that. Of course, it's also important to enjoy learning together. Use your best judgment about whether these activities will work for your children.

With a little adaptation, these lessons and activities can be used by a large or small Primary, class, or family. For example, instead of picking one or two children to volunteer, you may want to let every child in your group have a turn. You will need the Spirit's guidance to help you adapt your planning to fit the children you serve. Remember that each one is a child of God and each one wants to be included. If you have children with different abilities or special circumstances, do your best to be sensitive to their needs, even if it means changing your original plans.

Please note that this book is not meant to supersede or take precedence in any way over the Church's curriculum. It simply contains some additional ideas for busy teachers and parents. Whether you use it in your home, at church, or in another setting, I hope it will be a helpful resource to you so that you can spend your limited time focusing on the children you love and the eternal principles they need to learn.

Chapter 1: January

I WANT TO RETURN TO MY HEAVENLY FATHER

MULTIMEDIA RESOURCES

"I Am a Child of God," YouTube video, 2:54, posted by "Mormon Channel," May 11, 2011, www.youtube.com/watch?v=JOrcqqpHCt8.

"God Is Our Father," You Tube video, 3:05, posted by "Mormon Channel," August 10, 2011, www.youtube.com/watch?v=H0y2G0hpZK8.

"Going to Grandma's," YouTube video, 4:02, posted by "Mormon Channel," February 21, 2017, www.youtube.com/watch?v=11GgH0Kmc2I.

"Introduction: Our Heavenly Father's Plan," YouTube video, 4:07, posted by "Mormon Channel," January 3, 2012, www.youtube.com /watch?v=UukuRsECBkE.

SONG LIST

- **"I Am a Child of God" (2)**
- "I Lived in Heaven" (4)
- "I Will Follow God's Plan" (164)
- "Teach Me to Walk in the Light" (177)

GOSPEL ART BOOK

Christ and Children from around the World (no. 116)

Week 1: God Is My Heavenly Father

SCRIPTURE

Articles of Faith 1:1

TALK

When Alma the Younger was a young man, he did not want to listen to his father, who was the prophet. Alma the Younger made trouble for the Church, and he did not believe in Jesus. But Alma the Elder never stopped loving his son. Alma the Elder prayed that Alma the Younger would learn the truth and make good choices. One day, an angel appeared and told Alma the Younger to repent. The angel said that Heavenly Father had heard Alma the Elder's prayers for his son.

Each one of us has a father like Alma the Elder. It is our Heavenly Father. Our Heavenly Father loves us even if we make bad choices. He hopes that we will repent so that we can return to live with Him someday.

Alma the Younger did repent. He gained a testimony of Jesus and became a powerful prophet like his father. We can become more like our Heavenly Father when we make good choices. Our Heavenly Father knows each one of us. He created our spirits and our bodies. He sent us to earth to learn how to become like Him. Each day, He blesses us with the things we need because He loves us so much.

LESSON

DISCUSSION: Tell the children that this year in Primary, you will be talking about someone who loves them very much. This person is Heavenly Father. Ask the children what they already know about Heavenly Father. Invite a few teachers or members of the Primary presidency to join you at the front of the room and take turns sharing answers to the following questions:

- How do we know that Heavenly Father loves us?
- Why is it important to know that we are children of God?
- How does knowing that you are a child of God change how you see yourself and your choices?
- What are some ways we can develop a closer relationship with our Heavenly Father?
- How can we show Heavenly Father that we love Him?

ACTIVITY: Read the lyrics of the song, "I Am a Child of God" (2), pausing occasionally and asking the children what word comes next. Repeat this activity with the lyrics to the song, "My Heavenly Father Loves Me" (228). Point out the important doctrines that these songs teach us about our relationship with our Heavenly Father.

APPLICATION AND REVIEW: Testify that you know that Heavenly Father loves His children and that He wants us to love one another and return to live with Him someday. Share how you have gained a testimony of Heavenly Father's love for you and how you know that Heavenly Father loves each of the children in your Primary as well.

Week 2: Heavenly Father Has a Plan for Me

SCRIPTURE

Moses 1:39

TALK

Naya was excited when Elsie's mom asked Naya to help her plan a surprise birthday party for Elsie. Naya wanted everything to be perfect for her friend, so she told Elsie's mom exactly what kind of cake to get and which games to play at the party. On Elsie's birthday, Naya was so excited she had a hard time keeping the secret. After school, she helped to decorate Elsie's house while Elsie and her dad went shopping.

The party was a success! Elsie was so surprised, and she loved the cake and party games. When it was time for Naya to leave, Elsie gave Naya a big hug and thanked her for helping to plan the surprise party.

Whenever we want to do something well, it's important to have a plan. Plans help us decide what to do next; they make sure we don't forget anything. Heavenly Father has a plan for each one of us. His plan is not a surprise, like Elsie's party. We can learn about His plan in the scriptures. Because of Heavenly Father's plan, we always know what to do next, and we know that no one will be forgotten. Heavenly Father wants all of us to follow His plan so we can all return to Him someday.

LESSON

DISCUSSION: Explain to the children that before we were born, we lived with Heavenly Father. He wanted us to learn how to become more like Him. He had a plan for us, but Satan had another plan. We chose to follow Heavenly Father's plan and come to earth.

ACTIVITY: Tell the children that Heavenly Father's plan has three different parts. Write the words "Premortal Life" on the board, and explain that the first part of the plan happened before we were born. Write the words "Mortal Life" on the board, and tell the children that the second part of the plan is happening now. Then write the words "Postmortal Life" on the board, and explain that the third part will happen after we die. Divide the children into three groups and assign each group one part of the plan. Have the groups discuss their parts for a few minutes with the help of teachers or leaders. Then invite a few children from each group to stand and explain their part of the plan, starting with the premortal life, then mortal life, and then the postmortal life.

APPLICATION AND REVIEW: Help the children understand that Heavenly Father gave us His plan because He loves us. His plan helps us to know what is most important. By following His plan, we show Heavenly Father that we love Him and want to be like Him. Encourage the children to think about specific ways that they could follow Heavenly Father's plan this week and throughout the year.

Week 3: Heavenly Father's Plan Brings Us Joy

SCRIPTURE

2 Nephi 2:25

TALK

There are lots of things that make Luke happy and there are some things that make him sad. Luke feels happy when he gets to play in the water, when he gets to eat a yummy treat, or when he gets to go on vacations with his family. He feels sad when he gets hurt, when he makes a mistake, or when it's time to go to bed and he's not done playing.

Jesus explained that here on the earth there will be lots of things that will make us happy, but there will be other things that will make us sad. The things that make us sad are called trials or tribulations. But we don't need to be too sad because Jesus has overcome all of the tribulations in our world.

He has also prepared a better place for us to live with Him after we die. If we follow His plan and try to be like Him, we will be happy here on earth and, eternally, after we die. That is why we sometimes call Heavenly Father's plan the plan of happiness. Following His plan will make us happy forever.

LESSON

DISCUSSION: Tell the children that Heavenly Father knows we will make mistakes. If we repent when we make a wrong choice, His plan will help us to be happy again. We can follow His plan by trying to choose the right. Ask the children what it means to have joy or what makes them feel joyful. Explain that while we will not be happy all the time in this life, joy is the happiness that we will feel eternally as we follow God's plan.

ACTIVITY: Help the children memorize 2 Nephi 2:25. Repeat the verse and scripture reference several times together. Then, once most of the children have learned the verse, point to a line of children or go around the room and have each child say one word in the verse and reference. If a child cannot remember the next word, fill it in yourself. Do this until the children do not miss a word.

APPLICATION AND REVIEW: Remind the children that one of the things that brings us joy is our families. Ask the children how they could encourage the other members of their families to follow God's plan so that they can be together forever. Share some things that bring you joy and encourage the children to strive to follow the plan of happiness.

Week 4: I Can Choose for Myself

SCRIPTURE

2 Nephi 10:23

TALK

Jesus told a story about a young man who made some bad choices. Instead of staying with his family and working, the young man used all of his money to travel, buy fancy clothes, and go to big parties. When his money was gone, the young man had nothing left. He had no home, no friends, and almost no food to eat. His bad choices had made him very sad.

The young man decided to return home and ask his father for a job. He hoped that his father would let him work and try to make up for his bad choices. As soon as his father saw the young man coming, he ran out to meet him. The father was so happy to have his son back that he celebrated with all of his friends and family. The young man knew that he had made a good choice to come home.

This story is a parable because we are all like the young man. When we make bad choices, we go farther away from our Heavenly Father and this makes us sad. But when we repent and choose the right, we become closer to Heavenly Father and that makes us happy. Our good choices make Heavenly Father happy too. He wants each of us to repent and return to Him, and the only way we can do that is by following His plan. Jesus helps us repent and make good choices each day so that we can live with our Heavenly Father forever.

LESSON

DISCUSSION: Explain to the children that Heavenly Father sent us to earth so that we could learn how to choose the right. Here we are able to make all kinds of choices. Ask the children to name some choices they have made in the past few months. Point out that we are free to choose between good and bad, but that every choice we make has a consequence.

ACTIVITY: Tell the children that the scriptures are full of examples of people who made choices. Some people made good choices and were blessed. Others made bad choices and were not blessed.

Write the names from the following chart on the board. Have the children choose one name at a time. Read or summarize the scriptures listed for this person. Ask the children what choice this person made and what the consequence of that choice was. Use the chart to guide your discussion.

PERSON	SCRIPTURES	CHOICE	CONSEQUENCES
Noah	Genesis 6:13–14, 22	Build an ark	Saved from the flood
Abraham	Genesis 22:2–3, 10–13	Obey God and sacrifice his son	Blessed by the Lord and given a ram to sacrifice instead
Esau	Genesis 25:29–34	Sell his birthright	Was not given the priesthood
Esther	Esther 5:1–3	Risk her life to save her people—the Jews	Saved her family and her people
Laman and Lemuel	1 Nephi 17:18–19, 53–54	Murmur, complain, and not help Nephi build the ship	Shocked and shaken by the Lord
The brother of Jared	Ether 1:35	Pray to the Lord	He and his family could still understand each other
Emma Smith	D&C 25:2–3	Be faithful and help Joseph	Blessed and given special callings

APPLICATION AND REVIEW: Remind the children that every choice we make has a consequence. Some consequences come right away and others come later. Tell the children about a time when you were blessed for choosing the right. Testify that Heavenly Father wants to bless us each time we make a good choice.

Chapter 2: February

THE EARTH IS WHERE WE LEARN TO FOLLOW JESUS

MULTIMEDIA RESOURCES

"Our Earth, Our Home—God Created the Earth For Us to Enjoy & Take Care Of," YouTube video, 1:34, posted by "Mormon Channel," June 20, 2014, www.youtube.com/watch?v=cGxYvos1DMw.

"God's Greatest Creation," YouTube video, 2:51, posted by "Mormon Channel," October 11, 2013, www.youtube.com/watch?v=dMZ-ETxj0hE.

"Spiritual Whirlwinds," YouTube video, 2:24, posted by "Mormon Channel," March 7, 2017, www.youtube.com/watch?v=DzWXSz9hlxw.

"The Sting of the Scorpion," YouTube video, 2:50, posted by "LDS Youth," August 26, 2011, www.youtube.com/watch?v=XZCQHPGT78o.

SONG LIST

- "I Feel My Savior's Love" (74)
- "Keep the Commandments" (146)
- "The Lord Gave Me a Temple" (153)
- **"My Heavenly Father Loves Me" (228)**
- "I Think the World Is Glorious" (230)

GOSPEL ART BOOK

The Earth (no. 3)

Week 1: Jesus and Heavenly Father Created the Earth

SCRIPTURE

Genesis 1:1, 31

TALK

Parker likes to build things, draw pictures, and act out stories that he thinks up in his mind. Parker's mom always tells Parker that he has a great imagination and that he's a very creative kid. If you are creative, it means that you create things, or you make them.

Each of us has the ability to create something. Some people create things with their hands. Others create things with their minds. And others create good relationships by being kind and loving. Creating means taking some elements that were there before and arranging them in a way that is better or different.

Jesus and Heavenly Father are also creative. They created the earth for us so that we would have a good place to live. They created the mountains and the oceans and the sky. They created animals and fish and all the grass and trees and flowers. And They did all this because They love us so much. We can show that we love Them too by being thankful for all that They have given us, by taking good care of Their creations, and by creating beautiful things ourselves, just like our Heavenly Father and Jesus.

LESSON

DISCUSSION: Explain to the children that it took a long time for Heavenly Father and Jesus to create the earth. The scriptures refer to these periods of time as days, and on each day certain things were created. Read or paraphrase Genesis 1 and have the children hold up the corresponding number of fingers each time you read about a new day.

ACTIVITY: Invite the children to use their own creativity to draw a picture of something Heavenly Father and Jesus created. It might be a picture of their favorite spot in nature or their favorite animal or their favorite kind of weather.

APPLICATION AND REVIEW: If time permits, invite a few children to bring their drawings to the front of the room and show them to the other children. Encourage the children to share their drawings with their families and to remember to thank Heavenly Father for His creations in their prayers this week. Ask them how else they can show gratitude for Heavenly Father's creations.

Week 2: Adam and Eve Chose Righteously

SCRIPTURE

2 Nephi 2:11

TALK

Bailey and Brynlee are sisters, but they are not the same. Bailey loves summertime, playing sports outside, and going to the beach. Brynlee loves wintertime when she can snuggle up inside, drink hot chocolate, and read stories. Just like summertime and wintertime, our world is full of opposites.

In fact, our world needs opposites to make it work. We need daytime when we can work and nighttime when we can rest. We need cold weather and hot weather, and sunshine and rainy days to help things grow. Heavenly Father knew we would need all of these things. He created these opposites for us.

He also knew that we would have to learn how to choose between good and evil. Heavenly Father did not create evil, but He allows Satan to tempt us so that we can learn the difference between good and bad things. When we make wrong choices, Heavenly Father wants us to repent. And when we choose righteously, He is happy. Bailey and Brynlee are not the same, but they do agree that it is good to choose the right.

LESSON

DISCUSSION: Ask the children if they know who Adam and Eve are. Explain that Adam and Eve were the first people to live on the earth. All of us are descended from them, and their choices had a lasting effect on our world.

ACTIVITY: Read the story of Adam and Eve (below) to the children. Have them raise their hands each time Adam or Eve make a choice.

Jesus and Heavenly Father created a beautiful world for us to live on. But they had not created any people yet. Then they created Adam. He was the first man on the earth. Adam could not live by himself, so Heavenly Father and Jesus also created Eve. Adam and Eve lived in a beautiful garden called Eden. They were happy there. They got to decide what names to use for all of the animals. They were able to eat lots of yummy fruits and vegetables. But there was one tree whose fruit they were not allowed to eat. Heavenly Father had told them not to eat this fruit. If they did, they could not live in the Garden of Eden anymore.

Satan tried to tempt Adam and Eve to eat the fruit. At first, they would not listen. But Satan kept trying. Eventually, Eve chose to eat the fruit. She knew that Heavenly Father had told them not to eat it, but she also knew that eating the fruit would mean she could learn new things. Even though she loved living in the Garden of Eden, she knew it was time to leave. In the garden, everything was good all the time, but Adam and Eve needed to experience more than just good things if they were going to grow and become more like Heavenly Father.

After Eve ate the fruit, Adam ate it too. Heavenly Father told them that they had to leave the Garden of Eden, so Adam and Eve left. Outside of the garden, it was harder to work for their food and the other things they needed, but Adam and Eve chose to stay together. They made many decisions about where to live, how to worship, and what tasks they would do each day. In time, Adam and Eve had many children, and they taught their children about Jesus and Heavenly Father.

APPLICATION AND REVIEW: Emphasize the fact that Adam and Eve's choices allowed us all to come to earth. Point out that when they lived in the Garden of Eden, Adam and Eve's choices were limited. Only after they ate the fruit, left the garden, and experienced our world with all of its opposites, were they able to choose for themselves and use their full agency. Explain to the children that Jesus and Heavenly Father knew that Adam and Eve would eat the fruit. They prepared a way for Adam and Eve to repent and return to live with Them again someday.

Week 3: I Came to Earth to Get a Body and Learn to Choose the Right

SCRIPTURE

Alma 34:32

TALK

Before we were born, we lived with Heavenly Father. We were spirits, but we did not have our bodies yet. There were many things we could learn about as spirits, but there were some things we could not learn without our bodies. Heavenly Father and Jesus created the earth as a place for us to come and be tested. They created bodies for us to live in on earth.

Now that we have bodies, there are many wonderful things we can learn with them. We can learn how yummy brownies are because we can taste them. We can learn how cold snow is because we can feel it. We can learn about the beautiful smells of different kinds of flowers because we can smell them. We can also learn how to work hard, how to keep our bodies healthy, and how to make sure we stay clean.

I am glad to have a body. I use my body every day to learn and grow. There are many things here on earth that I can do with my body. I know Heavenly Father is happy when I make good choices and take care of my body.

LESSON

DISCUSSION: Ask the children to share some of their favorite sights, smells, sounds, tastes, and feelings. Point out that we can experience all of these things because we have bodies. Our bodies are gifts from Heavenly Father. He sent us here to earth so that we could learn how to take care of our bodies. While we are here on earth, we will be tested. If we choose the right, we will be able to return to live with Heavenly Father and Jesus someday.

ACTIVITY: Watch the video, "God's Greatest Creation," posted by the Mormon Channel on YouTube (www.youtube.com/watch?v=dMZ-ETxj0hE). Have the children listen and watch for all of the miraculous things our bodies can do. List these on the board.

APPLICATION AND REVIEW: Explain to the children that while we are here on earth, we will all experience things that will test us. Some of these tests will be physical challenges, others will be thoughts in our minds, and others will happen in the world around us. This is part of living on earth. Encourage the children to see these tests or trials as opportunities to show Heavenly Father that we want to choose the right.

Week 4: I Can Learn to Keep the Commandments

SCRIPTURE

Alma 37:35

TALK

When Jesus lived on the earth, He taught His followers many things. He taught them what was right and what was wrong. Jesus said that there were two great commandments. The first commandment was to love Heavenly Father. The second commandment was to love our neighbors. Our neighbors are all of the people around us, not just the people who live close to us.

There are many ways to show Heavenly Father that we love Him. Some of the ways to keep this commandment are to keep the Sabbath day holy, attend church, pay tithing, read the scriptures, pray, and be reverent. There are also many ways to love our neighbors. We could keep this commandment by being kind to others, giving service, being honest, and saying nice things to people so that they know we care about them.

It is important to keep the commandments because that is how we show Heavenly Father that we want to do what is right. If we keep the commandments, make good choices, and live righteously, we can return to be with Heavenly Father someday. The commandments show us how to become more like Him and how to follow His plan while we are here on earth.

LESSON

DISCUSSION: Ask the children to help you think of some rules that should be part of your Primary. The rules might include things like being reverent during lessons, singing along to the songs, or raising a hand and waiting to be called on before speaking. Explain that commandments are rules that we have been given by Heavenly Father. He gives us commandments because He loves us and wants us to be safe and happy. Obeying the commandments is how we show Heavenly Father that we love and honor Him.

ACTIVITY: Hold up one of the following pictures from the *Gospel Art Book* and ask the children to guess the commandment that the picture illustrates. Once they have guessed correctly, ask them how that commandment helps us to be happy or avoid a negative consequence. Repeat this activity with all of the pictures, displaying them on the board as you discuss them. As a variation on this activity, you could hide the pictures around the room or under certain chairs and discuss the pictures as the children find them.

PICTURE	COMMANDMENTS
Daniel Refusing the King's Food and Wine (no. 23)	We have been commanded to keep the Word of Wisdom.
John the Baptist Baptizing Jesus (no. 35)	We have been commanded to be baptized by immersion like Jesus was.
The Good Samaritan (no. 44)	We have been commanded to love and serve one another.
Joseph Smith Seeks Wisdom in the Bible (no. 89)	We have been commanded to read the scriptures.
Young Boy Praying (no. 111)	We have been commanded to pray always.
Payment of Tithing (no. 113)	We have been commanded to pay tithes and fast offerings.
Salt Lake Temple (no. 119)	We have been commanded to go to the temple and do family history work.

APPLICATION AND REVIEW: Encourage the children to think about all of the different commandments they learned about today and any other commandments they know. Have them each choose one commandment to focus on specifically this week. Ask them how they could better keep that commandment; tell them that you will invite them to report on their progress the following Sunday.

Chapter 3: March

JESUS HELPS ME RETURN TO HEAVENLY FATHER

MULTIMEDIA RESOURCES

"I'm Trying to Be Like Jesus," YouTube video, 5:16, posted by "Mormon Tabernacle Choir," May 6, 2014, www.youtube.com/watch?v=oe2HZuEZG6I.

"Jesus Is Resurrected," YouTube video, 4:05, posted by "Mormon Channel," April 7, 2012, www.youtube.com/watch?v=MlKetn7ZiNU&t=27s.

"The Shiny Bicycle," YouTube video, 3:04, posted by "Mormon Channel," August 15, 2013, www.youtube.com/watch?v=ItEsXGhcOEs&t=7s.

SONG LIST

- **"If the Savior Stood Beside Me"***
- "He Sent His Son" (34)
- "Beautiful Savior" (62)
- "I'm Trying to Be like Jesus" (78)
- "Help Me, Dear Father" (99)

* (available online at LDS.org or in the October 1993 edition of the *Friend* magazine)

GOSPEL ART BOOK

Jesus Praying in Gethsemane (no. 56)

Week 1: I Can Follow Jesus

SCRIPTURE

John 13:15

TALK

Kassie and Sabelle love volleyball. They are on the same team, and they work hard and practice together so that they can improve their skills. They both love their coach; she is really good at volleyball! She shows them how to pass the ball, serve, set, and hit. When Kassie and Sabelle want to get better at volleyball, they watch their coach and try to do exactly what she does. Their coach also watches them so that she can help correct them if they make mistakes.

Just like Kassie and Sabelle, we all have a coach. Our coach is Jesus Christ, and He helps us as we try to become more like Heavenly Father. We can learn how to become better people by learning about Jesus and doing what He did. Jesus set a perfect example for us to follow. He showed us how to be kind to others, how to show respect and love for Heavenly Father, and how to share the gospel.

If we try to do the same things that Jesus did, we will become more like Him. Jesus is also watching over us. He sees the mistakes we make, and because He loves us, He will help us correct our mistakes by repenting. As we follow the example that Jesus set, He will bless us and give us more opportunities to become better.

LESSON

DISCUSSION: Remind the children of their commitments from the previous Sunday and invite them to share how they tried to keep the commandments during the previous week. Explain that Jesus kept every commandment perfectly. He was perfect; so when we follow Him, and do what He did, we will naturally keep the commandments as we become more like Him.

ACTIVITY: Before your lesson, make a small puzzle that features a picture of the Savior. Obtain two identical pictures of the Savior. Leave one picture intact as the example to help the children solve the puzzle. Cut the other picture up into several puzzle pieces. Invite one child at a time to come to the front of the room, choose a puzzle piece, and share one thing that Jesus did to set a good example for us. Then have the child place the puzzle piece in the correct place on the puzzle, using the example picture as a guide. Continue until the puzzle is complete.

APPLICATION AND REVIEW: Point out that it was easier to complete the puzzle by looking at the example picture. In the same way, it is easier for us to keep the commandments when we look at the example set for us by Jesus. Encourage the children to continue learning about Jesus so that they will know how to keep the commandments.

Week 2: Jesus Atoned for My Sins

SCRIPTURE

Articles of Faith 1:3

TALK

One time when Moses was leading his people through the wilderness, many of them were bitten by poisonous snakes. Moses prayed for a miracle to help the people. Jesus wanted the people to remember that they needed to rely on Him. He told Moses that He would heal the people. All they needed to do was look at Moses's staff, which had a brass snake on it.

Many of the people did look at the staff, and they were healed. But some people did not believe that Jesus would heal them. They refused to look at the staff, and they remained sick. Some of them even died.

Later, when Nephi told this story to his family, he explained that the staff in this story was a symbol of Jesus Christ and His Atonement. The Atonement is the event where Jesus suffered for our sins so that we wouldn't have to suffer for them ourselves. When we use the Atonement, it is like we are looking at the staff in the story of the Israelites; Jesus Christ can heal us with the Atonement, just like the staff in the story. We use the Atonement when we repent. This means that we admit that we did something wrong and we try to do our best to make it right. There was only one way for the Israelites to be healed. They needed to look at the staff. And there is only one way for us to be healed spiritually. We need Jesus Christ and His Atonement in order to be clean and pure so we can return to live with Heavenly Father.

LESSON

DISCUSSION: Tell the children about a time when you made a mistake and needed to repent. (Your example should not be a serious transgression; choose something simple, like getting angry or telling a lie.) Explain that when we make mistakes, we feel sad inside. This feeling is often the Holy Ghost prompting us to repent so that we'll feel better.

ACTIVITY: Help the children understand what it means to repent by reading the following situations out loud, and then asking the children what the person or people in the story should do to repent.

- Emilee took her sister's favorite sweater without asking and wore it to school. At recess, Emilee was playing with her friends when she tripped and fell down in the mud. Her sister's sweater got all muddy. Emilee felt terrible. She knew her sister would be mad. What should she do to repent?
- One of Connor's chores is to unload the dishwasher every morning, but one morning he forgot and his mom had to do it for him. Connor felt bad that his mom had to do extra work when she was already very busy. What should he do to repent?

- Ethan and Sarah love going out to eat with their parents. One time, they found a wallet underneath a chair in a restaurant. Ethan said they should take the wallet and split the money between them. Sarah wasn't sure. She went along with Ethan's plan, but later, she felt bad about it every time she saw that money. What should they do to repent?
- Cassidy and Claire are neighbors. They used to be friends with a girl named Lindsay, but Cassidy and Lindsay had a fight. Now Claire only plays with Cassidy, and when Lindsay asks to play with them, they don't talk to her. Sometimes Claire sees Lindsay playing by herself and Claire feels bad because Lindsay looks lonely. What should she do?
- Oliver's mom made cookies one night and told Oliver that he could have one cookie before bedtime. But Oliver snuck back into the kitchen while his mom was helping his little sisters get ready for bed. He ate three more cookies from the jar. The next day, Oliver's mom didn't say anything about it, but Oliver felt bad. What should he do?

APPLICATION AND REVIEW: Explain that when we repent we feel happy and are filled with peace. Repentance is not always easy, but it helps us to return to Heavenly Father. Sing the song, "He Sent His Son" (34) with the children and explain that Heavenly Father sent Jesus Christ to earth so that He could die for our sins. When we repent, we are able to use Jesus's Atonement to help us become clean again. Encourage the children to continue thinking about ways they could use the Atonement to repent and improve.

Week 3: I Will Be Resurrected like Jesus

SCRIPTURE

Matthew 28:5–7

TALK

Spring is Joshua's favorite season. He loves to watch the snow melt as the sun begins to warm the earth and the air. He loves how the rain makes the flowers grow and how it makes the grass turn from brown to bright green. He loves being able to play outside with his friends without having to wear his heavy winter coat. He loves seeing the baby ducklings at the pond in the park.

Spring is a season of rebirth. Baby animals are born, and plants become active again after being dormant or asleep during the wintertime. We often think of these things in nature as symbols of how Jesus died, was buried, and then came back to life again.

This event was called the Resurrection. During the spring and at Easter, we celebrate Jesus's Atonement and Resurrection. Joshua loves Easter too. He knows that it is a special time for us to remember what Jesus has done for us. Because Jesus died and was resurrected, each one of us will be resurrected too. That means we will be able to live again after we die. We are blessed to know that death is not the end. Each one of us will live again. Jesus was resurrected and someday we will be too.

LESSON

DISCUSSION: Explain to the children that Jesus was the first person to be resurrected. This means that after He died, He came back to life. His body and His spirit were reunited, and He was alive again. Ask the children how it makes them feel to know that Jesus was resurrected. Tell them that because Jesus overcame death, we will all be resurrected too. Discuss how we are blessed by the knowledge that death is not the end and that we will live again in perfect, resurrected bodies.

ACTIVITY: Read Doctrine and Covenants 88:15, or ask a child to read it. To help the children understand what it means to be resurrected, pass out pieces of paper for them to color on. Have them fold their papers into three sections and draw lines to divide the three parts. In the first section of the paper, have them draw something that represents their spirits. Remind them that they were spirits before they were born. Label the line that divides the first and second sections of the paper, "Birth." In the second section of the paper, have the children draw a picture of themselves or a picture of the earth. Label the line between the second and third sections of the paper, "Death." In the third section of the paper, have the children draw a picture of what they will look like after they have been resurrected.

APPLICATION AND REVIEW: As the children are drawing, emphasize the fact that our bodies and spirits are eternal. We were created in the image of our Heavenly Father, and we will still look like ourselves when we are resurrected, but our bodies will be perfect—free from disease and other things that can harm us while we are living on the earth. Share your own feelings about the Resurrection and how your daily actions are affected by having an eternal perspective.

Week 4: Jesus Saves Us from Our Sins

SCRIPTURE

Mosiah 27:29

TALK

Max's dad has a big job to do. His dad works as a veterinarian at an animal hospital. Many of the animals he sees are badly hurt. They need help, and Max's dad is the one who helps them. No matter what has happened to the animals before they come to the hospital, Max's dad does his best to help them get better or to keep them from being in pain. Max thinks that his dad's job is pretty cool. His dad gets to save animals! Max loves his dad, and Max tries to help animals too.

Another person that Max loves is Jesus. Jesus had a big job to do too. He worked hard to save each one of us from our sins. Without His help, we would feel hurt, hopeless, and afraid. But because Jesus has atoned for our sins, we don't have to feel sad about them. Jesus has saved us from those sad feelings; all we need to do is rely on Him and repent. Jesus is the only one who can help us when we have sinned. No matter what we have done, Jesus still loves us and wants us to return to Him. Max thinks that what Jesus has done for us is very special. Max tries to help others learn more about Jesus so they can feel better too.

Each one of us has been saved by Jesus. That is why we call Him our Savior. He suffered for us so that we would not have to suffer if we truly repent. We can show Jesus that we are grateful for His saving power by telling others about how happy we feel when we repent, by loving others even when they make us sad, and by forgiving them when they have done something wrong. We are so blessed by what Jesus has done for us.

LESSON

DISCUSSION: Tell the children about a time when you or someone you know fixed or repaired something that was broken. Explain that this broken object was saved by being fixed. If it had not been fixed, it would have been thrown away or left to sit unused. Discuss how this is similar to what the Savior has done for each of us. Because He has saved us from our sins, we can try to live better lives. We can work hard to help others, instead of wasting our time feeling sorry for ourselves or dwelling on our mistakes.

ACTIVITY: To illustrate why we need a savior, invite one child to come to the front of the room. Tell the other children that this child is going to act as a balance.

Explain that when we sin, our lives are not balanced. In one hand, have the child hold a paper with the word "Justice" written on it. Tell the children that when we sin, we must be punished. That is an eternal law, and because Heavenly Father is eternal and fair, He cannot break this law. Have the child at the front of the room lean to one side to indicate that justice is heavy and would pull us off-balance.

Now hand the child another paper with the word "Mercy" written on it. Explain that mercy is something that is given to us by the Savior when we repent. Mercy allows Jesus to be punished instead of us. In order to access this mercy, we must rely on Jesus by repenting. Have the child at the front of the room lean toward the center to indicate that mercy balances out justice.

Explain that because Jesus atoned for our sins, the eternal law of justice remains satisfied. But we do not have to suffer because Jesus has suffered for us.

APPLICATION AND REVIEW: Bear your testimony to the children that Jesus is our Savior, and that He is the only one who can atone for our sins and help us return to our Heavenly Father. Encourage the children to talk about this subject with their families and to thank Heavenly Father in their prayers for sending His Son to save us.

Chapter 4: April

JESUS GAVE US HIS CHURCH FOR OUR DAY

MULTIMEDIA RESOURCES

"The Restoration," YouTube video, 3:00, posted by "LDS Youth," April 13, 2016, www.youtube.com/watch?v=_MzDz7OXKUE.

"Mormon Church: The Message of the Restoration," YouTube video, 2:22, posted by "Mormon Channel," February 6, 2009, www.youtube.com /watch?v=ySyv1I2e9RE.

"Ministry of Mormon Prophet—Joseph Smith: The Restoration of Priesthood Authority," YouTube video, 1:20, posted by LDS Church History, August 13, 2014, www.youtube.com/watch?v=Hm4Iye76nlo.

"Ministry of Mormon Prophet—Joseph Smith: The Book of Mormon," YouTube video, 1:19, posted by LDS Church History, September 2, 2014, www.youtube.com/watch?v=8RnFVW1j_os.

SONG LIST

- The Church of Jesus Christ (77)
- The Golden Plates (86)
- On a Golden Springtime (88)
- Book of Mormon Stories (118)
- I Will Be Valiant (162)

GOSPEL ART BOOK

The First Vision (no. 90)

Week 1: The True Gospel Was Lost

SCRIPTURE

2 Thessalonians 2:3

TALK

Henry and Mason love to help their mom make their grandma's special cinnamon rolls. They always make cinnamon rolls around Christmastime and for special family parties during the rest of the year. But they didn't used to make cinnamon rolls like they do now.

When Henry was small and Mason was just a baby, their mom never made cinnamon rolls because their grandma had lost the recipe. Their mom tried to remember all the ingredients and how much of them to use, but somehow her cinnamon rolls never turned out exactly right. So she stopped trying. Then one day, their mom got a phone call. Their aunt Lucie had found the recipe hidden in their grandma's kitchen. The whole family was excited! They could finally enjoy those special cinnamon rolls again!

The gospel is much more important than a recipe for cinnamon rolls. But after Jesus died, many of the important gospel truths He had taught were lost or changed, like the lost cinnamon roll recipe. The disciples tried to keep records, like recipes, that would help them remember what Jesus had taught them, but a long time passed and the records did not last. That was why Jesus needed to appear again in our day. He came to earth with Heavenly Father to teach Joseph Smith the true gospel. Now that we have the truth again, we can enjoy the gospel exactly as Jesus taught it to His disciples.

LESSON

DISCUSSION: Explain to the children that Jesus's gospel was perfect while He lived on the earth. He established a church in His day. But over time, His church and His gospel were changed. A very long time passed before Jesus revealed His true Church to Joseph Smith.

ACTIVITY: Play a game of Telephone to illustrate how gospel truths can change or be altered over time. Invite several children to the front of the room and have them stand in a line. Whisper one of the example sentences below in the ear of the child at one end of the line, then have each child in the line pass along the whispered words. Have the last child in the line say the words they are told out loud. Compare these words to the words you whispered to the first child.

Example sentences:

- Joseph Smith prayed to know the truth about which church to join.
- All of the apostles tried to preach the gospel.
- Some people wanted to confuse Christians or change the Church.
- When Jesus revealed the true church to Joseph Smith, this was called the Restoration.

APPLICATION AND REVIEW: Emphasize how blessed we are to have the fulness of the gospel in our day. Discuss some of the specific doctrines that Joseph Smith helped restore, such as the nature of the Godhead or temple covenants and ordinances. Share how grateful you are for the restored gospel.

Week 2: Joseph Smith Saw Jesus and Heavenly Father

SCRIPTURE

Joseph Smith—History 1:17

TALK

When Joseph Smith was a young boy, his family often discussed religion. They believed in Jesus Christ and they tried to follow Him. But the Smith family could not agree about which church was the true church that Jesus wanted them to join. In that time, many of the leaders of different churches liked to argue with each other so that they could prove that their church was right and that other churches were wrong. This was not what Jesus taught. He taught us to be kind, and not to argue.

As Joseph grew older, he listened carefully to the leaders of the different churches, and he read the Bible often. He also talked with his parents and his brothers and sisters to see what they thought about Jesus. All Joseph wanted was to do what was right. He wanted to follow Jesus, but he was not sure which church would help him to do that the best.

Eventually, after thinking and pondering for a long time, Joseph read an important verse of scripture. This scripture is in the book of James. The scripture said that if we need to know something, we should use our faith to ask God and He will tell us what we need to know. Joseph decided to do just that; he would ask God. When Joseph prayed, he received a miraculous answer. Jesus and Heavenly Father appeared and told Joseph that none of the churches were correct. All of the work that Joseph had done to try to find the answer himself had prepared him to learn the truth.

Today, when we need to know something, we can work hard to find the answer ourselves. When we ponder and read the scriptures, Heavenly Father will help us learn the truth.

LESSON

DISCUSSION: Display the picture The First Vision (no. 90), from *the Gospel Art Book*. Ask the children if they know what this picture depicts. Invite one of the older children or a teacher to give a brief summary of the First Vision. (You may want to have a child or teacher read the talk listed above as a way to begin your discussion.)

ACTIVITY: Watch the video, "The Restoration" posted by "LDS Youth" on YouTube (www.youtube.com/watch?v=_MzDz7OXKUE&t=82sF). Then ask the children the questions below. (If some children have trouble remembering or understanding the video, you may want to play it again. Or you can ask the children who do understand to summarize what the video means in their own words. This will help the others understand the video better and answer the questions.)

1. Why did the gospel need to be restored?
2. Who did Jesus and Heavenly Father appear to in order to restore the gospel?
3. What role did the Book of Mormon play in the Restoration?
4. How many apostles were in Christ's ancient Church, and how many do we have today?
5. What is Jesus's role? Has His role changed since He lived on the earth?

APPLICATION AND REVIEW: Point out that the First Vision was a very special occasion because Heavenly Father does not usually appear to us when we pray. Encourage the children to gain their own testimonies of the Restoration by praying and asking Heavenly Father to help them know the truth. Tell them that even though their experience will probably not involve a vision, Heavenly Father will help them to know what is good and true, just as He helped Joseph Smith learn the truth.

Week 3: The Priesthood Has Been Restored

SCRIPTURE

D&C 124:123

TALK

Dalton's dad is the bishop of their ward. This means that often on Saturdays or other times during the week, his dad needs to stop by the church building to get something from the bishop's office or check on things around the building. Dalton likes to go with his dad when he goes to the church. His dad lets him use a special key that opens all of the doors in the building.

We have another kind of key in our Church. It is not a key you can hold in your hand. It is a power from Heavenly Father. He gives us these keys or powers so that we can do the work that He would do if He were here. These special keys from Heavenly Father are called priesthood keys. Dalton's dad has some of these keys because he is a bishop.

When Dalton is a little older, he will also receive priesthood keys as he advances in the priesthood. The prophet is the only person on earth who holds and can use all of the priesthood keys from Heavenly Father. But these keys have not always been on the earth. For a long time after Jesus died, these keys were lost. We are blessed to have these priesthood keys in our Church. They are a great gift from Heavenly Father because they help us make covenants and perform ordinances that will let us return to Him.

LESSON

DISCUSSION: Remind the children that after Jesus died, His true Church was changed and lost. One of the biggest things that was lost was the priesthood. Explain that the priesthood is the power of God and that we need this power in order to perform ordinances like baptisms and enter into eternal covenants like marriage. Show the children a family history chart that illustrates the link between several generations. Explain that just as we can trace our family history back into the past, we can also trace the power of the priesthood as it was given to priesthood holders. Ask the children who the first person on the earth was (Adam). Explain that if we traced our family history back to the very beginning, all of our charts would start with Adam. The same thing is true of the priesthood. Each priesthood holder's authority can be traced back to Jesus and Joseph Smith. Jesus conferred the Aaronic and Melchizedek Priesthoods on special leaders who gave those priesthoods to Joseph Smith in our day. Joseph then conferred these priesthoods on others and the power of God spread and spread. Now it stretches around the world.

ACTIVITY: Read the accounts of the Aaronic and Melchizedek priesthood restorations and have the children illustrate these events (see Joseph Smith—History 1:68–72). You may also wish to display the following pictures from the *Gospel Art Book*: John the Baptist Conferring the Aaronic Priesthood (no. 93) and Melchizedek Priesthood Restoration (no. 94). Make sure the children understand who was present in each instance, and why it was necessary for Joseph to receive priesthood power and authority from these special messengers.

APPLICATION AND REVIEW: Help the children understand that our Church is different because we have the priesthood, and we have been authorized to use the power of God on the earth. Share your feelings about the restoration of the priesthood. Testify that the priesthood blesses all of us—both those who hold it and those who enjoy the blessings it brings into our lives. If time permits, invite the children to share ways that the priesthood has blessed them or their families.

Week 4: The Book of Mormon Helped Restore Lost Truths

SCRIPTURE

2 Nephi 3:12

TALK

Eva's family is bilingual. That means that they speak two languages. Some members of her family only speak English, and some of them only speak Spanish. Eva knows both. Because Eva can speak two languages, she can help people understand each other when they don't speak the same language.

When one of Eva's grandmas comes to visit, she mostly speaks in English. But Eva helps her grandma understand the Spanish words they use. When Eva visits her other grandparents, they mostly speak Spanish, and Eva helps them understand English. This is called translating.

Joseph Smith used the priesthood to help him translate the Book of Mormon. He did not know the ancient language that the record was written in. So he had to ask Heavenly Father for help. Heavenly Father knows all of our languages. He helped Joseph understand what was written on the gold plates. Joseph had friends who helped him write down the words that he received from Heavenly Father. Eventually, those words became the Book of Mormon that we read today.

LESSON

DISCUSSION: Ask the children if they know how we received the Book of Mormon. Summarize in your own words what happened between the time that the angel Moroni first appeared to Joseph Smith and when the translation of the Book of Mormon was complete. Make sure the children understand that this work was miraculous and could not have been completed without Heavenly Father's help.

ACTIVITY: Give each class a coded message to "translate" from the chart below. Display the key at the front of the room or distribute copies of this key to each class. Younger classes will need the help of a teacher or leader. (For a printable version of this activity, visit primaryhelper.com.)

CODED MESSAGES	TRANSLATION
1. DXQLAV QOWHV GLQHXGLI HLOAFL XGIWESENLQ HVSH NSE YWEI XTG ZSOWFWLQ HXBLHVLG ZXGLJLG.	1. Joseph Smith restored temple ordinances that can bind our families together forever.

CODED MESSAGES	TRANSLATION
2. DXQLAV QOWHV GLQHXGLI HVL MLRQ XZ HVL AGWLQHVXXI SEI HVL STHVXGWHR HX SNH WE BXI'Q ESOL.	2. Joseph Smith restored the keys of the priesthood and the authority to act in God's name.
3. DXQLAV QOWHV HGSEQFSHLI AXGHWXEQ XZ HVL YWYFL QX UL NXTFI TEILGQHSEI UVSH HVLR OLSE.	3. Joseph Smith translated portions of the Bible so we could understand what they mean.
4. DXQLAV QOWHV HGSEQFSHLI HVL YXXM XZ OXGOXE, UVWNV HLQHWZWLQ XZ NVGWQH.	4. Joseph Smith translated the Book of Mormon, which testifies of Christ.
5. DXQLAV QOWHV XGBSEWCLI HVL NVTGNV WE HVL QSOL USR NVGWQH XGBSEWCLI WH WE VWQ ISR.	5. Joseph Smith organized the Church in the same way Christ organized it in His day.
6. DXQLAV QOWHV GLJLSFLI HVL UXGI XZ UWQIXO, UVWNV HLSNVLQ TQ VXU HX NSGL ZXG XTG YXIWLQ.	6. Joseph Smith revealed the Word of Wisdom, which teaches us how to care for our bodies.

KEY

A	B	C	D	E	F	G	H	I	J	K	L	M
P	G	Z	J	N	L	R	T	D	V	X	E	K

N	O	P	Q	R	S	T	U	V	W	X	Y	Z
C	M	Q	S	Y	A	U	W	H	I	O	B	F

When all of the classes have finished translating their messages, have one person from each class read the message to the other children and display it on the board. Then discuss why it was important for this part of the gospel to be restored, and how we are blessed by having it in our lives.

APPLICATION AND REVIEW: Bear your testimony of Joseph Smith and the sacred work that he did to restore the true church. Emphasize how blessed we are to have the true church again on the earth and the fulness of the gospel in our day. Encourage the children to share what they have learned about the Restoration with their families and friends.

Chapter 5: May

I CAN FOLLOW THE PROPHET

MULTIMEDIA RESOURCES

"Priesthood Keys: The Restoration of Priesthood Keys," YouTube video, 2:08, posted by "Mormon Channel," April 19, 2013, www.youtube.com /watch?v=CKnBNeHrw4M.

"Follow the Prophet," YouTube video, 4:16, posted by "LDS Youth," April 3, 2015, www.youtube.com/watch?v=AM8aBrgsxfg&t=13s.

"Continue in Patience," YouTube video, 2:41, posted by "Mormon Channel," September 28, 2010, www.youtube.com/watch?v=654QGjYHlJY&t=14s.

"We Need Living Prophets," YouTube video, 2:44, posted by "Mormon Channel," October 18, 2012, www.youtube.com/watch?v =j8nSv95wXyM&t=74s.

SONG LIST

- Follow the Prophet" (110)
- "Latter-day Prophets" (134)
- "I'm Glad to Pay a Tithing" (150)
- "The Word of Wisdom" (154)

GOSPEL ART BOOK

Thomas S. Monson (no. 137)

Week 1: We Have a Living Prophet

SCRIPTURE

Mosiah 8:16

TALK

Scott's family lives far away from a church building. Most of the time on Sundays, they have to get up early so they can get ready and drive a long way to get to church. Scott knows that church is important, and he likes going to Primary and sacrament meeting, but he wishes there was a closer church building so they wouldn't have to get up so early.

That is one of the reasons why Scott loves general conference. On conference weekend, his family doesn't have to wake up early because they get to have church at home. Scott's family uses their computer to watch general conference online. It is almost like having all of the church leaders come over for a visit in their home!

The other reason that Scott loves general conference is that he gets to listen to the prophet. Scott knows that the prophet is a very important person. Our prophet tells us the things that Jesus wants us to hear today. We are blessed to have a living prophet to lead our Church. Each time we listen to the prophet and try to do what he says, we will become better people and we will make Heavenly Father and Jesus very happy.

LESSON

DISCUSSION: Tell the children that today you are going to be talking about someone very special; it is our prophet. Ask the children if they can name the prophet. Then ask them if they know what he does. Discuss why it is important to have a living prophet. Make sure the children know that this is something that sets our Church apart from many others. We believe that the prophet is the only person with the power and authority to speak for Heavenly Father in matters that concern the Church and its members.

ACTIVITY: Explain that a prophet is like a link between us and Heavenly Father. Read Amos 3:7, or ask an older child to read it. This verse tells us that the Lord will do nothing without revealing His plans to His prophet.

Pass out small strips of paper to the children. Have them write or color something on each strip that the prophet has told us to do. When the children are done, have them stand up—one at a time—and share what the prophet has told us to do. It is all right if many of the children have the same answer. As the children share their answers, use tape to form a paper chain with the strips of paper, making links in the chain. When your chain is complete, display it at the front of the room.

APPLICATION AND REVIEW: Tell the children that just as there are links in the chain, the prophet's words link us to Jesus and Heavenly Father. We can keep that connection strong by following the prophet's counsel. Encourage the children to think of ways that they can follow the prophet each day so they can stay connected to Heavenly Father and Jesus Christ.

Week 2: Our Prophet Leads the Church

SCRIPTURE

D&C 107:92

TALK

McKenzie is learning to play the clarinet in the orchestra at school. In an orchestra, there are many different instruments that all play different parts. Every person playing has to pay close attention to the conductor so that all of the parts come together correctly.

McKenzie knows that she needs to learn her music well enough to look at the conductor and not at her notes. She spends a lot of time practicing on her own at home so that she will be ready for her rehearsals with the whole orchestra at school.

In our Church, we have millions of members, but we only have one prophet. A prophet is like the conductor in an orchestra. He makes sure that all of the different parts of the Church work well together. Each of us must pay close attention to what the prophet says so that we can live the gospel the way Jesus wants us to.

There are some things in the gospel that we can practice on our own, like saying our prayers or reading our scriptures. It is important to do these ourselves so that when we come to church, we are ready to learn from our prophet and our other leaders. Even though he is very busy, our prophet loves each one of us. He knows how much Heavenly Father loves us, and he wants to help us feel that love each day as we live the gospel and choose the right.

LESSON

DISCUSSION: Ask the children why it is important to have a leader. Explain that in our Church, Jesus Christ is our leader. Jesus has given us a prophet to act in His name and to be our leader here on the earth. The prophet tells us what Jesus wants us to know right now.

ACTIVITY: To illustrate the importance of having a leader, give the children a simple task to accomplish, like gathering papers from around the room and putting them in two equal stacks. The first time, have them try to accomplish the task without any leadership. After they are done, have them try the task again, but this time choose five or six children to be the leaders. The leaders should tell the other children what to do, but encourage the leaders to talk over one another or to create confusion by giving conflicting commands. Repeat the task a third time, but this time, choose only one leader.

APPLICATION AND REVIEW: When the children are done, have them return to their seats. Ask them if it was easier to do the task with no leaders, with lots of leaders, or with only one leader. Point out that Heavenly Father has organized His Church with just one leader—our prophet. While the prophet has counselors, apostles, and other good men and women to help him, he is the only one who is authorized to speak for Jesus and Heavenly Father. That is why it is so important to listen when He gives us commandments or instructions. Bear your testimony of the importance of having a living prophet to lead and guide our Church.

Week 3: Our Prophet Teaches Us to Pay Tithing

SCRIPTURE

Malachi 3:10

TALK

One day, Caleb and Lia saw a cool new game at the toy store. They asked their mom if she would buy it for them, but she said that they would need to earn the money themselves. When they got home from the store, Caleb and Lia put their money together, but there was not enough to buy the game.

Then Caleb had a great idea. He told Lia they should sell lemonade outside their house to help them earn more money for the game. Lia liked that idea. She helped Caleb make the lemonade and a sign so people would know how much to pay. Caleb and Lia sold lots of lemonade that day, and they kept selling more the next day and the day after that. Eventually, they thought they had enough money to pay for the game. Then their mom reminded them that they needed to pay tithing on the money they had earned. Caleb and Lia counted out their tithing money and put it in an envelope. But now they didn't have enough money to buy the game.

The next day was Saturday. Caleb and Lia set up their lemonade stand again, and soon they had lots of customers. They made so much money selling lemonade that day that they were able to pay their tithing, buy the game, and still have enough money to buy a treat on the way home. Caleb and Lia knew they had been blessed for paying their tithing.

LESSON

DISCUSSION: Ask the children to name some of their blessings. Encourage them to think of all that Heavenly Father has given them. Then ask them what we can give back to Heavenly Father. Explain that the prophets have taught us to pay our tithing. Paying our tithing is one way that we give back to Heavenly Father. When we pay our tithing, we make a small sacrifice that leads to big blessings.

ACTIVITY: To help the children visualize how small one-tenth is compared to all that Heavenly Father has given us, set up several stations around the room where the children can measure out one-tenth of something. You could use popcorn kernels, beans, rice, papers, clay, or even water. Have a teacher or leader at each station to show the children how to measure. If you are worried about a potential mess, have the children stay in their seats and invite one or two to come forward and measure out one-tenth while the other children watch.

APPLICATION AND REVIEW: Make sure the children understand that we pay our tithing because we love Heavenly Father, and we want to obey the prophet. We do not pay tithing because we expect to receive blessings in return. But we will be blessed when we are obedient to the prophet's counsel to pay tithing and make wise decisions with our temporal resources.

Week 4: Our Prophet Teaches Us the Word of Wisdom

SCRIPTURE

D&C 89:18–19

TALK

When Jacob and Will were little, they did not like vegetables. They only wanted to eat treats, snacks, and desserts—not healthy things. Their parents often became angry when the boys would not cooperate at dinnertime. Then one day, their mom taught them a special lesson at family home evening. She explained that the prophets have taught us to keep the Word of Wisdom.

The Word of Wisdom is a special commandment from Heavenly Father that helps us take care of our bodies. It teaches us to eat good foods and to not eat foods that are unhealthy. It also teaches us not to smoke or drink bad drinks. Jacob and Will listened carefully. They wanted to obey the Word of Wisdom because they knew that it would make their parents and Heavenly Father happy.

Now Jacob and Will do eat vegetables. There are still some vegetables that they don't like, but there are others that they like a lot. They both try hard to obey the Word of Wisdom and eat the things they know will help their bodies. Jacob and Will want to take good care of their bodies so they can show Heavenly Father that they are grateful for the bodies He has given them.

LESSON

DISCUSSION: Explain to the children that our prophets have taught us many things. Tell the children you are thinking about one thing in particular that our latter-day prophets have taught us to follow. Have the children guess what that thing is. If necessary, give them additional hints until they guess the Word of Wisdom.

ACTIVITY: Read Doctrine and Covenants 89 out loud to the children. Encourage them to listen carefully by having them stand up each time they hear the word "body" or "bodies." When they hear something that is good for us to eat or drink, have them raise their hands and then write that item on the board. When they hear something that is not good for us to eat or drink, have them shake their heads. When you finish the section, ask the children to explain what you read in their own words.

APPLICATION AND REVIEW: Help the children understand that the Word of Wisdom is a warning. It helps us keep our bodies free from addictions and disease. Conclude by reiterating some of the special blessings that are promised to us when we keep the Word of Wisdom. Encourage the children to follow the prophets by always living the Word of Wisdom.

Chapter 6: June

I CAN BE BAPTIZED AND CONFIRMED

MULTIMEDIA RESOURCES

"Baptism: A Bible Story for Children," YouTube video, 3:13, posted by "Mormon Channel," June 1, 2016, www.youtube.com/watch?v=yBX7wM1pn4Y&t=10s.

"Jesus Is Baptized by John," YouTube video, 2:54, posted by "Mormon Channel," May 11, 2012, www.youtube.com/watch?v=9_dr9njVzKM&t=8s.

"The Last Supper," YouTube video, 6:01, posted by "Mormon Channel," April 6, 2012, www.youtube.com/watch?v=997ni1xcmKw.

"Not a One Time Thing—Atonement," YouTube video, 3:00, posted by "Mormon Channel," December 1, 2012, www.youtube.com/watch?v=bvn7Q2RnSoc.

SONG LIST

- To Think about Jesus (71)
- This Is My Beloved Son (76)
- Baptism (100)
- **When I Am Baptized (103)**
- Listen, Listen (107)

GOSPEL ART BOOK

Girl Being Baptized (no. 104)

Week 1: I Can Be Baptized like Jesus Was

SCRIPTURE

Matthew 3:16–17

TALK

Marea loves her two older brothers. She wants to do everything that they do. Even though she is little, she runs as fast as she can to keep up with them. She always joins in with their sword fights, and pretends to be a pirate with them when they go to the beach. Marea doesn't know how to read yet, but she listens carefully when her brothers read during family scripture study.

Marea's brothers set a good example for her to follow. She wants to be just like them when she gets older—including being baptized. One of Marea's brothers was baptized a few months ago, and she loved watching his baptism.

When Marea's brother was baptized, he was following the example set by Jesus. Jesus was baptized while he lived on the earth. He went to the Jordan River, where his cousin John was teaching and baptizing. Jesus was baptized by immersion, which means he went all the way under the water. That's how Marea's brother was baptized too. And someday, that is how she will be baptized. Marea is excited to follow her older brothers' example and be baptized in the same way that Jesus was. She wants to follow the example of her older brothers and make good choices, and all three of them want to follow the example of Jesus.

LESSON

DISCUSSION: Explain to the children that Jesus was perfect. He did everything exactly right. That means that if we do everything that He did, we will always choose the right too. Have the children list some things that the Savior did while He lived on the earth. Then ask them how they could do those same things themselves. Point out that one of the things that Jesus did while He lived on the earth was get baptized. He did this to set an example for us so that we would know how to be baptized ourselves.

ACTIVITY: Watch the video, "Baptism: A Bible Story for Children," posted by the "Mormon Channel" on YouTube (www.youtube.com/watch ?v=yBX7wM1pn4Y&t=10s). After the video, ask the children the same question that was asked in the video: "Why are we baptized?" Point out some of the answers that were in the video. With younger children, encourage them to talk about why they want to be baptized someday. And with older children, give them an opportunity to talk about when they were baptized and to share their feelings about that experience.

APPLICATION AND REVIEW: If you feel prompted, share the story of your own baptism. Tell the children how you felt on that day, and how you have felt in the time since, as you have reflected on that experience. Help them understand that baptism is an important step on their journey back to Heavenly Father, and that the covenants they make when they are baptized will help them strengthen their relationship with Him and with Jesus Christ.

Week 2: I Can Listen to the Holy Ghost

SCRIPTURE

John 14:16

TALK

Drew's grandpa knows about lots of different kinds of birds that live in the woods near their home. When they go bird watching, they always bring a notebook to record what they find. But Drew's grandpa says that the most important thing they bring is their ears. Their ears help them listen for birdcalls—way up in the high branches of the trees.

Drew's grandpa recognizes all the different birds by the different calls they make. He can tell when the birds are scared or are about to fly away. It is almost like he has learned a different language. Drew is trying to learn to hear the birds the way his grandpa can.

Another thing Drew's grandpa is teaching him is how to listen to the language of the Holy Ghost. The Holy Ghost teaches us in different ways. We call these teachings promptings. Drew's grandpa has explained that sometimes a prompting comes as a thought in your mind. If this happens, it can help to record the thought or write it down, so that you don't forget it later—just like Drew and his grandpa keep a record of the birds they see. Other times, the Holy Ghost might prompt us with a feeling when we are reading the scriptures, listening to a friend talk, praying, or just thinking. Drew's grandpa is helping him to understand how to recognize these promptings and learn the language of the Spirit, so that Drew will know when the Holy Ghost wants to tell him something.

LESSON

DISCUSSION: Ask the children to name some of the best gifts they have ever received. Explain that Heavenly Father gives each one of us a gift when we are baptized in His Church. This gift is the gift of the Holy Ghost. The Holy Ghost is a wonderful gift because He can help us return to Heavenly Father. When we have the gift of the Holy Ghost, we can know what Heavenly Father wants us to do and how He wants us to do those things.

ACTIVITY: Display the picture Boy Samuel Called by the Lord (no. 18) from the *Gospel Art Book*. Tell the children that often when we receive a prompting from the Holy Ghost, we do not recognize it at first. Invite a few children to come to the front of the room and act out the story of Samuel being called by the Lord in 1 Samuel 3:1–11. You will need at least two volunteers to help—one to be Samuel and one to be Eli. You could also ask an older child to read the scriptural account or act as a narrator. To involve more children, you could invite all the children watching to act as the voice of the Lord and call to Samuel three times.

APPLICATION AND REVIEW: Explain that even though we may never hear the voice of the Lord calling to us, we will blessed with specific promptings or messages from the Holy Ghost. We need to prepare for these messages and obey the promptings we receive. Testify that the Holy Ghost will always be there to help, comfort, guide, and protect us.

Week 3: I Can Take the Sacrament

SCRIPTURE

Matthew 26:26

TALK

Jirene was baptized when she was eight, but now that she is eleven that seems like a long time ago. She can remember how good she felt then, and sometimes she wishes she could be baptized again so that she could feel clean and happy like she did that day. When she asked her parents about being baptized again, they told her that she could soon go to the temple and perform baptisms for the dead. But Jirene wasn't sure that being baptized for someone else would feel the same as her own baptism did.

Then Jirene's mom told her something she did not know. Her mom explained that we don't need to be baptized again because we can renew our baptismal covenants when we take the sacrament. Each week, we have the chance to become clean again just like when we were baptized.

The sacrament is the most important part of our church meetings. It is a time when we can feel the Spirit and think about how we felt when we were baptized. We can prepare for the sacrament by trying our best to repent. We can also prepare by practicing being reverent. Now Jirene is trying to make each Sunday as special as her baptism day. She knows that when we have repented and are reverent during the sacrament, it can bless our lives every week, and we can grow closer and closer to Heavenly Father and become more and more like Him.

LESSON

DISCUSSION: Explain to the children that the sacrament is a sacred time when we can show Heavenly Father and Jesus Christ that we love Them and want to do the right things. When we are baptized, we make promises to Them.

The sacrament is a time for us to think about those promises and how we are doing at keeping them. If we have made mistakes, the sacrament is a good time to think about how we can fix those mistakes so that we can become better. Most of all, the sacrament is a time to remember Jesus and the sacrifice that He made for us. He suffered and died for us, so that we would not have to suffer for our own sins.

ACTIVITY: Teach the children to sing one of the sacrament hymns in the hymnbook. Explain the words and the doctrines behind them as you are learning the song together. Try to choose a hymn that your ward sings frequently so that the children will recognize it and be able to sing along when they hear it again.

APPLICATION AND REVIEW: Tell the children that it is very important to be reverent during the sacrament so that others can feel the Spirit. Ask them how they could be more reverent or what kinds of things they could do to keep themselves focused on the Spirit during that part of the meeting. Share your thoughts and feelings about what helps you to stay focused during the sacrament, and how you use that time to reflect on Jesus Christ, His Atonement, and your own covenants.

Week 4: I Can Repent and Be Forgiven

SCRIPTURE

Helaman 13:11

TALK

Zeezrom was not nice to people who believed in Jesus. But Heavenly Father knew that Zeezrom could become a good person if someone helped him to see the truth. Heavenly Father sent Alma and Amulek to preach the gospel in the city where Zeezrom lived. At first, when Zeezrom met Alma and Amulek, he did not believe what they were preaching.

Zeezrom tried to trick Alma and Amulek into saying something wrong. Normally, he was very good at this, because his job was to trick people into saying the wrong thing. Alma could not be tricked though. The Spirit helped him to know what Zeezrom was thinking.

Eventually, Zeezrom realized that what Alma and Amulek were saying was true. Zeezrom felt terrible about how he had tried to trick people. He knew that he needed to repent, but he was so sad. He did not think that Jesus and Heavenly Father would want him to be part of their Church.

Alma knew how that felt. He had once been wicked himself. Alma gave Zeezrom a blessing that helped him to feel better. Now Zeezrom knew what

Heavenly Father had known all along—he could be a good person. He needed Jesus Christ and His Atonement to help him, and Jesus did help Zeezrom. In time, Zeezrom became a good leader and a good missionary. He tried to help others learn to repent just like he had, so that they could be happy like he was.

LESSON

DISCUSSION: Show the children a rock that has been smoothed down by being in the water. If you do not have a rock to show them, use a picture. Explain that this rock was once rough, but over a long period of time, the water has taken off all of the rough edges and left the rock smooth. You may wish to pass the rock around for the children to touch. Help the children understand that we can become like this rock. Our mistakes are like rough spots on the rock, but as we repent and try to live righteously, Heavenly Father and Jesus Christ can help us change so that we become smooth or perfect, with no more rough edges. The process of repenting is like the water that smooths away those rough edges. We do not become perfect all at once; it takes time. But little by little, we can become more and more like Jesus. And because He loves us, He will forgive us each time we truly repent.

ACTIVITY: Pass out papers to the children. Have them draw a sad face on one side of the paper. Then have the children fold the paper in half with their sad face on the inside of the fold. On the blank side of the paper that is now showing, have the children draw a few things that make them happy. Explain that we feel sad when we make a mistake. Sometimes that mistake is all we can think about and it's hard to feel happy, because we know that Heavenly Father is not pleased with what we have done. But as we repent and are forgiven, we become clean again. Then we can stop feeling sad and enjoy all the things that make us happy.

APPLICATION AND REVIEW: Help the children understand that Heavenly Father always wants us to repent so that we can be forgiven. We are His children and He loves us no matter what mistakes we make. Encourage the children to always repent when they make mistakes so that they can be forgiven and become more and more like Jesus.

Chapter 7: July

A FAMILY IS FOREVER

MULTIMEDIA RESOURCES

"Families Can Be Together Forever," YouTube video, 3:10, posted by "Mormon Channel," February 8, 2011, www.youtube.com/watch?v=0J-_f4oRuWI.

"Temples Are a Beacon," YouTube video, 2:50, posted by "Mormon Channel," January 23, 2012, www.youtube.com/watch?v=73jY8xH_vhc.

"My Brother Hyrum," YouTube video, 2:41, posted by "Mormon Channel," April 23, 2013, www.youtube.com/watch?v=OWU6UbGgmT4.

SONG LIST

- "I Love to See the Temple" (95)
- **"Families Can Be Together Forever" (188)**
- "Family Prayer" (189)
- "Love Is Spoken Here" (190)

GOSPEL ART BOOK

Family Prayer (no. 112)

Week 1: Families Are Part of Heavenly Father's Plan

SCRIPTURE

1 Nephi 8:12

TALK

Abraham and Sarah were very old. They had prayed all their lives that they would be able to be parents. The Lord had promised them that someday they would be parents, but no children came. Abraham and Sarah were righteous. They would have been good parents. But the Lord had a plan for Abraham and Sarah's family. They just needed to trust in Him.

Each of us has been sent to a family. The Lord knows each one of us and our families. As part of His plan of happiness, He has sent us to the family that is right for us. The people in our family help us learn and grow. Some families are big and others are small. Every family is different and special.

After a long time, Abraham and Sarah were blessed with a son. They named him Isaac, and he became a great man. The Lord had fulfilled His promise. He had created a family for Isaac, and for Abraham and Sarah. Heavenly Father has always planned for us to come to earth and be part of a family. In our families, we learn to love one another in the same way that our Heavenly Father loves us. If we make good choices, we can live with our families eternally.

LESSON

DISCUSSION: Show the children a picture of a temple. Ask them whose house it is. Explain that the temple is a sacred place where we can feel the Spirit. Then show the children a picture of a home. It could be a photograph of your home or the home of someone else in the ward. Ask the children whose house is in the picture. Explain that, just like the temple, our homes are sacred places where we can feel the Spirit. We can help to make our homes happy, peaceful places by being kind to the people in our family.

ACTIVITY: Before the lesson begins, use a pad of sticky notes or paper and tape to place the following questions under some of the chairs in the room.

- Who is in your family?
- How can you show your family that you love them?
- What makes your family special?
- What does your family like to do together?
- Where is one of your favorite places to go as a family?
- What are some of your favorite memories you have made with your family?
- How can you show Heavenly Father that you are grateful for your family?
- What kind of food does your family like to eat?
- What kind of music does your family like to listen to?
- What do you like best about your family?

Invite the children with papers under their chairs to come to the front of the room and answer the question on the papers they have found.

APPLICATION AND REVIEW: Point out that the children's answers from the activity show that every family is different. Heavenly Father knew that not every family would be the same. He sent us to our unique families so that we could have special experiences that we would not be able to have in any other way.

Have the children name some additional ways that they could show kindness and love to their family members. Encourage each of them to thank Heavenly Father in their prayers that night for sending them to a special family.

Week 2: Gospel Habits Help My Family

SCRIPTURE

1 Nephi 19:22

TALK

When Lehi and his family left Jerusalem, they knew that Heavenly Father had a plan for their family. They did not know everything that would happen on their journey, but they knew that they would be protected by Heavenly Father and would eventually be led to a promised land where they could live righteously.

Along the way, they learned many lessons about being obedient and listening to the Spirit. One day, Lehi found something special outside of his tent. It was called the Liahona and it showed them which way to go. But it only worked if they paid close attention to it and made good choices. When they were not obedient, the Liahona would not show them which way to go.

Each of us is part of a family. Most of our families are not on physical journeys, the way that Lehi's family was. But all of our families are on a journey back to our Heavenly Father. In order for us to move forward on our journey, there are certain things we can do as a family to be obedient and feel the Spirit. We can pray together, study the scriptures together, and have family home evening. As we live the gospel, we will have the Spirit in our lives to direct us—like a Liahona. The Spirit will help us as we get closer and closer to our Heavenly Father and all of the wonderful things He has in store for our families.

LESSON

DISCUSSION: Remind the children that Heavenly Father sent them to their families so that they could learn from each other and help one another. Explain that one way we can help our families is by encouraging each member in our family to live the gospel. We can do this by praying together, studying the scriptures together, having family home evening, going to church together, and keeping the Sabbath day holy as a family.

ACTIVITY: Have an older child or teacher read the following sentence from The Family: A Proclamation to the World: "Successful marriages and families are established and maintained on principles of faith, prayer, repentance, forgiveness, respect, love, compassion, work, and wholesome recreational activities."

Have each child draw a picture of their family members doing something together that will help them live the gospel.

APPLICATION AND REVIEW: Encourage the children to share their pictures with their parents and other family members and to display them in their homes during the upcoming week. Invite the children to encourage their families to live the gospel together by improving in the specific areas depicted in their pictures. You could even encourage them to set a small goal in that area with the other members of their families. For example, a child might draw a picture of studying the scriptures as a family. That child could help the family to improve their family scripture study by volunteering to get out the scriptures and call everyone to come for scripture study. A good family goal in that area might be to study the scriptures together as a family for fifteen minutes each day that week.

Week 3: The Priesthood Helps My Family

SCRIPTURE

James 5:14–15

TALK

Quinn's family lives in a good house. They have plenty of food to eat, clean clothes to wear, and toys to play with. Her family is blessed with lots of things that you can see, but even more important than those blessings are the invisible blessings that you can't see. Many of these invisible blessings come from the priesthood.

For example, Quinn's parents were sealed together in the temple when they got married. This special sealing means that Quinn's family will always be a family, even after death. This is a great blessing in their lives. It helps them to know that they will be together forever and that the love they feel now will stay with them.

Another blessing from the priesthood is that Quinn's dad can give her blessings when she's feeling sick or hurt or scared. A father's blessing is not something you can see, but it helps you feel better or more peaceful.

There are many blessings in our lives that we can see, but the invisible blessings in our lives, like the ones that come from the priesthood, are so special. These invisible blessings cannot be taken away from us, and they will continue to bless our families each day of this life and eternally.

LESSON

DISCUSSION: Explain to the children that the priesthood is a gift from Heavenly Father. It gives us the authority and power to do the things that He would do if He were here. The priesthood can help us heal the sick, direct the Church, and even perform miracles. The priesthood also blesses our families.

ACTIVITY: Invite a priesthood holder in your ward to come to Primary and talk to the children about how the priesthood blesses our families. Be sure to ask permission from the bishop before extending this invitation. Introduce the priesthood holder as a guest speaker and encourage the children to be reverent as he is speaking.

APPLICATION AND REVIEW: Emphasize the fact that all families are blessed by the priesthood, even families that do not currently have a priesthood holder in their homes. Encourage the children to thank the priesthood holders in their lives for exercising their priesthood worthily.

Week 4: Someday I Can Have My Own Eternal Family

SCRIPTURE

4 Nephi 1:11

TALK

When Joseph Smith was a young man, he met a young woman named Emma Hale. Joseph was staying with Emma's family while he worked for Emma's father. Joseph and Emma got to know each other well. They became good friends and after some time, they decided to get married.

Because Joseph was often busy organizing the true Church and helping other Church members, there were many times when Emma had to take care of their house and children all alone. Heavenly Father blessed their family, but they had to face many trials too. Through all of their trials, Joseph and Emma tried their best to love one another and help each other. They knew that no matter what happened, they were sealed together so their family would last forever.

In our Church, we know that we will each be given the opportunity to be sealed to our own eternal families. Eternal families are so important to Heavenly Father's plan. He wants to bless each one of us with a family that we can love and that will love us forever.

Not every family is perfect in this life. Many families face trials, like Joseph and Emma did. But no matter what happens in our lives or in our families, Heavenly Father will eventually work things out. We just need to be patient and keep making good choices. If you do this, your family will be always be blessed for your obedience and faith. Heavenly Father's plan is a plan of happiness, and one of the most important parts of that plan is a happy family that you can be with forever.

LESSON

DISCUSSION: Ask the children what they would like to be when they grow up. Point out that in addition to preparing for a job or preparing to serve a mission, they can begin to prepare now to be married in the temple someday. Help them understand that they will need to make righteous choices in order to be worthy to enter the temple. Ask them to share some things they could do now to prepare to be sealed in the temple.

ACTIVITY: Watch the video "Always in Our Sights—The Temple," posted by "Mormon Channel" on YouTube (www.youtube.com/watch?v=cBtZZIeeUIE). Encourage the children to stay focused on the temple. Encourage them to set a goal now to be worthy to enter the temple one day so that they can be sealed and begin their own eternal families.

APPLICATION AND REVIEW: Tell the children about how important the temple is in your life. Share with them the feelings you experience when you are there. Testify of the importance of eternal families to God's plan of happiness and the great blessings that come from being sealed to the people you love most.

NOTE: As you are teaching this lesson, be sensitive to those children, teachers, and leaders whose families may be struggling or whose family situations are not ideal. Emphasize that while we may experience trials related to our families in this life, Heavenly Father knows each of us and will bless us and our families as we do our best to choose the right.

Chapter 8: August

I CAN PRAY TO MY HEAVENLY FATHER

MULTIMEDIA RESOURCES

"Prayer," YouTube video, 4:12, posted by "Mormon Channel," January 11, 2010, www.youtube.com/watch?v=zndsJTdGwLQ&t=7s.

"Pure and Simple Faith," YouTube video, 5:30, posted by "Mormon Channel," January 10, 2012, www.youtube.com/watch?v=TDdde1Pi1lU&t=81s.

"He Knows Me—Godhead," YouTube video, 3:01, posted by "Mormon Channel," December 1, 2012, www.youtube.com/watch?v=CFXda8HWhyk.

"Having the Holy Ghost: Power of the Holy Spirit," YouTube video, 2:56, posted by "Mormon Channel," www.youtube.com/watch?v=u-4POloNEz0.

SONG LIST

- "A Child's Prayer" (12)
- "I Pray in Faith" (14)
- "Seek the Lord Early" (108)
- "Search, Ponder, and Pray" (109)

GOSPEL ART BOOK

Enos Praying (no. 72)

Week 1: I Can Learn How to Pray by Reading the Scriptures

SCRIPTURE

Matthew 6:6

TALK

Micah is learning how to say prayers. He already knows that when we pray we should fold our arms, bow our heads, and close our eyes. Micah is little, so right now when it is his turn to say the prayer, he just repeats the words that his mom says. As he gets older, Micah will learn how to say prayers all by himself.

Even though Micah is little and needs help praying, Heavenly Father still hears Micah's prayers. Heavenly Father knows that Micah is trying to talk with Him, and because Micah is one of His children, Heavenly Father loves to listen to Micah's prayers.

Heavenly Father loves to listen to all of our prayers. He wants to know how we are feeling and what things we need. Heavenly Father is full of love for each of His children. It makes Him so happy when we talk with Him about the things that we are doing and learning. In our prayers, we can thank Heavenly Father for all the blessings He has given us and ask Him to bless us with the things we still need.

LESSON

DISCUSSION: Show the children your phone or another device that you use to communicate. Tell them that we are blessed with many tools that help us to stay in touch with one another, but we do not need any of these devices to stay connected to our Heavenly Father. We can talk to Him anytime we want to by saying a prayer. Explain that the scriptures teach us about prayer and how to connect with our Heavenly Father each day.

ACTIVITY: Ask the children if they know what "question words" are. These are words that begin a question, like "who," "what," "where," "when," "why," and "how." When we ask questions, we can learn. Tell the children that today they are going to learn about prayer from the scriptures. Using the chart below, assign each class one of the question words and give them the scripture reference that corresponds with their word. You will also need to give each class a piece of paper. Instruct the classes to read their scriptures and then write the question word at the top of their piece of paper. Then have them use the rest of the paper to illustrate the answers that they find to their question word in the scriptures.

QUESTION WORD	SCRIPTURE VERSES
Who do we pray to?	3 Nephi 18:18–21
What does it mean to keep a prayer in your heart?	Mosiah 24:10–15
Where should we pray?	Alma 33:2–8
When should we pray?	Alma 37:36–37
Why are we told to pray always?	3 Nephi 20:1; D&C 10:5; D&C 19:38
How should we pray?	Matthew 6:9–13

When the classes have finished, have them present what they learned and the illustrations they drew on their papers to the other children.

APPLICATION AND REVIEW: Teach the children that there are many stories in the scriptures that teach us about prayer. Encourage the children to think of scripture stories that involve prayer. Help the children understand that prayer is their way to communicate with Heavenly Father. He wants them to pray to Him reverently, and He always hears and answers our prayers.

Week 2: I Can Pray Always

SCRIPTURE

2 Nephi 32:9

TALK

Alma and Amulek were missionaries. They wanted to teach the Zoramites, but the Zoramites had their own kind of church. The Zoramites had created a tower called a Rameumptom where they went to pray. Instead of praying during the week, they came every seven days to the Rameumptom, waited in a long line, climbed to the top, and then each person said the exact same prayer as every other person who came to pray.

Alma and Amulek knew this was not right. Heavenly Father has told us that we should not say the same prayers over and over again. When we pray, we should talk to Him just as if we were talking to another person, but a person who is very important.

Heavenly Father also wants us to pray always, not just once a week. What does it mean to pray always? It means that we pray often, no matter where we are or what we are doing. It also means that we think about Heavenly Father and try to keep the Spirit with us, even when we are not praying.

Heavenly Father hears our prayers. He wants us to pray to Him as often as we can so that He will be able to bless us with the things that we need. He loves each one of us, and He loves when we talk to Him in our prayers.

LESSON

DISCUSSION: Ask the children when we usually say prayers. Tell them about a time when you said a prayer at a time or in a place that was unusual. It may have been a quick prayer for safety as you were driving or a time when you were prompted to pray for a loved one. Explain that while there are certain times and places where we usually say prayers, there is never a place or time when we cannot pray and have Heavenly Father hear us. No matter where we are, Heavenly Father can hear us when we pray.

ACTIVITY: Listen to a recording of the song "I Pray in Faith" (14), available on LDS.org. Point out to the children that the important part of a prayer is the faith you have when you pray—not the time or the place where you pray. Ask the children what it means to pray in faith. Discuss some ways to increase our faith or to pray more sincerely. Sing "I Pray in Faith" together to reinforce your discussion.

APPLICATION AND REVIEW: Encourage the children to pray always and to do so sincerely and with faith. Emphasize that Heavenly Father hears all our prayers and wants us to pray to Him as often as we can.

Week 3: Heavenly Father Answers My Prayers

SCRIPTURE

Jeremiah 29:12

TALK

When her family moved, Lisa was worried about having to go to a new school. At her old school, she had lots of friends and she loved to play basketball at recess. At her new school, Lisa didn't know anyone that she could play basketball with.

Lisa's parents told her she could pray for help making friends. Her parents reminded her that they had prayed as a family to find a good house to move into, and Heavenly Father had helped them find the right one. The night before school started, it was Lisa's turn to pray. She asked Heavenly Father to help her know what to do at recess. She prayed that she would learn to like her new school.

On her first day, Lisa said another prayer in her mind as she walked onto the playground. Just then, she saw some of the kids from her class playing basketball. She asked if she could join them, and they said yes. Lisa had fun playing with her classmates, and after a few days, she had lots of new friends. Lisa knew Heavenly Father had answered her prayers.

LESSON

DISCUSSION: Begin the lesson by inviting one child to come to the front of the room to be interviewed. Explain to the other children that in an interview, one person (the interviewer) asks questions and the other person (the person being interviewed) answers the questions. Ask the child you are interviewing a few simple questions, like "What is your name?" "How old are you?" "What is your favorite animal?" Then have the child sit down. Explain that often when we pray, we wish that our prayers could be like interviews. We wish that we could ask Heavenly Father lots of questions and have Him answer us right away. But that is not how prayer works. Sometimes we receive immediate answers, but often Heavenly Father waits to reveal answers to us until we are ready to receive them. Emphasize the fact that though the answers to our prayers don't always come when we want them to, Heavenly Father always answers our prayers in the way that is best for us.

ACTIVITY: Remind the children that many people in the scriptures prayed and received answers. Get three paper bags and label them: "person," "prayer," and "answer." Use the chart below to fill each bag with slips of paper that match the entries in each column from the chart. Invite four children to the front of the room and have them choose papers from the "person" bag. Have these children read the name on their slip of paper. You may need to help younger children read the names. Have these children stand to one side "until their prayers are answered."

Next, invite two more children to come to the front of the room and choose one paper each from the "prayer" and "answer" bags. Have these children read their papers aloud. Ask the rest of the children to listen carefully to see if the prayer and answer match. If they do not match, have the children sit down and ask for two more volunteers. If they do match, have the other children identify which person matches the prayer and answer and tape all of the papers up in order on the board, including the "person" paper for the person whose prayer was answered. Then have those three children sit down. Repeat this activity, drawing new "prayer" and "answer" papers until all of the children who drew "person" papers have had their prayers answered.

NOTE: Depending on the time available, you may need to modify this game to make it end more quickly. You could do this by drawing the "prayer" and "answer" papers yourself and having the other children in the Primary identify which "person" each "prayer" and "answer" belongs to.

PERSON	PRAYER	ANSWER
Hannah	Prayed for a child.	She was blessed with a son named Samuel.
Nephi	Prayed to know how to obtain the brass plates.	The Spirit told him to kill Laban.
Joseph Smith	Prayed to know which church was true.	Heavenly Father and Jesus Christ told him that none of the churches were correct.

PERSON	PRAYER	ANSWER
Moses	Prayed for help to free his people from the Egyptians.	He used the power of God to part the Red Sea.
The brother of Jared	Prayed for light inside his boats.	The Lord touched sixteen stones and made them glow.

APPLICATION AND REVIEW: Share your own testimony that the Lord answers our prayers. Tell the children about a time when you prayed and received an answer from the Lord. Encourage them to look for the ways that Heavenly Father answers their prayers and invite them to discuss these ways with their parents and other members of their families.

Week 4: My Prayers Are Answered in Many Ways

SCRIPTURE

2 Nephi 4:35

TALK

Tyson and Emma love dinosaurs. They know about lots of different kinds. Some dinosaurs walked on the ground, some swam in the ocean, and others flew through the air. Tyson loves drawing pictures of all the different dinosaurs, and Emma likes pretending to be a dinosaur and reading books so she can learn more about them.

Just as there are lots of different kinds of dinosaurs, Tyson and Emma know that there are also lots of different kinds of answers to our prayers. Sometimes we receive an answer to our prayers right away as a good feeling or a thought we might not have had on our own. Other times, we need to study the scriptures and the words of the prophets to help us find the answers. Emma thinks this is kind of like the studying that scientists do when they want to learn more about dinosaurs.

Tyson and Emma know that Heavenly Father always answers our prayers, even if we do not recognize the answers we receive. Sometimes we need to be patient and wait for Heavenly Father to bless us at the right time. He knows us so well and He knows what we need. He will always take care of us and answer our prayers when we ask for good things.

LESSON

DISCUSSION: Ask the children if Heavenly Father has ever answered their prayers. Ask a few of them to describe how their prayers were answered. If the children cannot think of any specific ways in which their prayers were answered, ask their teachers to name some answers to their prayers. Point out that not all answers to prayers will look or feel the same.

ACTIVITY: Tell the children that we sometimes need to look harder in order to see how our prayers have been answered. This is a bit like being a detective. A detective is someone who looks for clues to figure out how or why something happened. Explain that, today in Primary, you are going to become prayer detectives.

Assign each class a scripture story from the list below. Have them work with their teachers to identify who prayed, what the person or people in the story prayed for, and how the prayers were answered.

- Exodus 14:10, 21–22, 26–27
- Daniel 6:10, 16–23
- Luke 1:5–7, 11–15, 57
- John 11:1, 5, 32, 38–44
- Enos 1:11–17
- Joseph Smith—History 1:14–19

If time permits, have the children draw a magnifying glass on a piece of paper. Then, inside the magnifying glass, have them draw ways that Heavenly Father might answer their prayers.

APPLICATION AND REVIEW: Encourage the children to continue to become better prayer detectives in the coming week by looking for different ways that Heavenly Father answers prayers. Explain that they will find more clues as they read and ponder the scriptures and as they talk with their parents and teachers. Emphasize the fact that Heavenly Father answers all our righteous prayers in the way that is best for us.

Chapter 9: September

I CAN SERVE GOD BY SERVING OTHERS

MULTIMEDIA RESOURCES

"The Old Shoemaker," YouTube video, 3:27, posted by "Mormon Channel," December 15, 2014, www.youtube.com/watch?v=pifDZ1hu6gY.

"The Coat: A Story of Charity," YouTube video, 2:07, posted by "Mormon Channel," December 9, 2011, www.youtube.com/watch?v=cp3IH8ZNviQ.

"Lessons I Learned as a Boy," YouTube video, 4:03, posted by "Mormon Channel," January 20, 2009, www.youtube.com/watch?v=naqX9iYE0V0.

"Pass It On," YouTube video, 2:17, posted by "Mormon Channel," February 14, 2012, www.youtube.com/watch?v=Tf0JeKDK8aA)

SONG LIST

- "Kindness Begins with Me" (145)
- "Go the Second Mile" (167)
- "When We're Helping" (198)
- "'Give,' Said the Little Stream" (236)
- "I Have Two Little Hands" (272)

GOSPEL ART BOOK

Service (no. 115)

Week 1: I Will Serve Others like Jesus Did

SCRIPTURE

Matthew 25:40

TALK

When Jesus was just beginning to preach, His mother, Mary, needed help with something. They were attending a wedding with many other people, and there was nothing left to drink except for regular water. Mary knew that Jesus could help her, so she told everyone around them to do exactly as He said.

Jesus told the people to fill up six water pots with water. Then, when they were filled, Jesus said to serve the water to the people at the wedding. Before the people drank the water, Jesus used His power to change it so that it did not taste like water anymore. It tasted good, like the best kind of drink they could have. This was a miracle.

Jesus performed many miracles in His lifetime. Each one was something that He did in order to help the people around Him, just like He helped His mother that day at the wedding. We do not need to perform miracles in order to follow Jesus's example and help the people around us. We can do that by being kind, doing nice things for those who are hurt or sick, and being generous and willing to share what we have with those who do not have enough.

Jesus taught us to love one another the way that He loved us. He is always pleased when we serve the people around us.

LESSON

DISCUSSION: Remind the children that Jesus set a perfect example for each of us to follow. Discuss some of the things that He did to set an example while He lived on the earth, such as being baptized. Then tell the children that Jesus also set an example for us in the way that He loved and served the people around Him.

ACTIVITY: Display the following pictures from the *Gospel Art Book* around the Primary room.

- Jesus and the Samaritan Woman (no. 36)
- Jesus Calms the Storm (no. 40)
- The Ten Lepers (no. 46)
- Jesus Raising Lazarus from the Dead (no. 49)
- Jesus Washing the Apostles' Feet (no. 55)
- Jesus Praying in Gethsemane (no. 56)

Divide the children into six groups and place one group at each picture station. Include a teacher or two with each group to help guide the discussion. At each station, have the teacher or one of the children summarize the event that the picture depicts, and explain whom Jesus was serving and what He did to serve.

Rotate the groups until every group has seen three or four pictures—depending on the amount of time you have available.

APPLICATION AND REVIEW: Invite the children to return to their seats. Explain that while they will likely not be called on to perform miracles like Jesus did, they can still serve others like He did. This might include being kind to those who others don't like or calming a stormy situation by bringing peace when things are tense or scary. Encourage the children to think of other ways that they could follow Jesus's example and serve those around them every day.

Week 2: I Will Serve Others like the Prophets and Apostles Do

SCRIPTURE

D&C 59:5

TALK

One Sunday, George and Julie had a special church meeting. Instead of going to Primary and sacrament meeting at their regular church building, their family drove a long way to get to a big auditorium where they were going to listen to an Apostle speak. On the way there, their mom explained that Apostles often travel to different parts of the world to check on how things are going in the Church. She said that they were very blessed to have the Apostle come to where they lived and invite everyone in that area to come and listen to his words.

When George and Julie heard the Apostle speak, they felt a warm feeling. They knew that the Apostle had been called by God. They could also tell that the Apostle loved them and wanted to help them. George and Julie left the meeting feeling good. They wanted to be more like the Apostles and help others learn about Jesus.

Their mom told them they could do this by serving. The prophet and apostles serve each one of us every day. Instead of going to regular jobs, their job is to take care of the Church, testify of Jesus, and make sure that the Church is helping those who need help. We are blessed to have a prophet and apostles on the earth. They serve us all in the same way that Jesus would if He were here.

LESSON

DISCUSSION: Tell the children that the scriptures teach us that we should serve with all our heart, might, mind, and strength. Ask the children if they know what those words mean. Explain that the important part of this scripture is that it teaches us to give everything that we have and everything that we can do to Heavenly Father so that He can use us to bless others.

Show the children some pictures of the Prophet and the Apostles and explain that prophets and apostles give all their heart, might, mind, and strength to

Heavenly Father's work. Talk about some of the specific things that the Prophet does to serve others. Help the children understand that we can follow the Prophet by serving the people around us.

ACTIVITY: Pass out papers to the children and have them fold the papers into four sections. In each section, have the children write the words, "heart," "might," "mind," and "strength"—with one word in each section. If the children are too young to write, have them draw symbols, such as a heart (for "heart"), an arm with muscles (for "might"), a person thinking (for "mind"), and a spirit (for "strength," to symbolize that we can serve others through our spiritual strength).

When the children have finished writing or drawing, ask them to share examples of ways that they could serve others that are specifically related to each section on their papers. For example, they could use their hearts to serve others by being kind and loving to someone new in their class at school.

APPLICATION AND REVIEW: Encourage the children to serve others and remind them that, as they do, they will be following the prophet. Have them take their papers with them to help them remember to serve with all their heart, might, mind, and strength.

Week 3: I Can Serve Heavenly Father When I Serve Others

SCRIPTURE

Mosiah 2:17

TALK

The scriptures tell us that one of the most important commandments is to love and serve Heavenly Father, but how can we serve Him when He is not here? Another scripture tells us the answer. This scripture was given to us by King Benjamin.

King Benjamin was a righteous king. He spent his whole life serving his people. At the end of his life, he gathered all of his people together so that he could speak to them. He told the people that he had tried to love and serve them his whole life. He wanted the people to realize that if their king had served them, they should also serve each other.

Then King Benjamin said that all of the service he had given to them was really service that he was giving to Heavenly Father. King Benjamin explained that when we serve others, it is like we are serving God. This is because Heavenly Father loves each of His children. He wants to bless them, and often the way that He blesses others is by sending some of His righteous children to help those who need help.

We can follow King Benjamin's example, and serve our Heavenly Father by loving and serving His children, or in other words, by loving and serving all of the people around us.

LESSON

DISCUSSION: Show the children the piano in your Primary room. Explain that this is called a musical instrument. An instrument is something that can be used by someone to make something happen. Ask the children to think of some other things that could be called instruments, such as the tools used by a construction worker, a doctor, or a scientist. Then tell the children that the scriptures say we should be instruments for our Heavenly Father. This means that He should be able to use us to do His work, and often His work involves blessing and serving others.

ACTIVITY: Read the following situations out loud to the children. You could also ask older children to take turns reading these situations. After each one is read, discuss how the person or people in the situation could be instruments in the Lord's hands.

- One day, Rianna's little brother, Joseph, lost his favorite toy at the park. Rianna helped him look all over for his toy, but they could not find it before they had to leave the park. Joseph was so sad. Rianna wanted to help her brother to be happy again.
- Tage knows that his mom is really busy right now. She is trying to help out with projects at his school, start her own business, and take care of Tage and his sisters. Tage feels like he should help his mom take care of some things around the house so that she has more time to do all the things she needs to get done each day.
- A new family is moving in next door to Kylie's house. It looks like they have a girl who is the same age as Kylie. It also looks like the parents in the new family are worried and busy trying to get everything moved in. Kylie is wondering if there is something she could do to help her new neighbors.
- One afternoon, Benjamin and Evelyn were planning to help their mom make cookies, but then their mom told them that instead of making cookies, she needed to make dinner for another family in the ward whose mom was sick that day. Benjamin and Evelyn were disappointed about the cookies, but they wanted to help their mom and the other family.
- Danny's dad works hard to provide for their family. Lately, when he gets home from work, he seems extra tired, sad, or even angry. Danny wants to help cheer him up or do something nice for him that will help him forget about his work for a little while.

APPLICATION AND REVIEW: Remind the children that there are opportunities to serve others all the time; we just need to listen to the promptings of the Holy Ghost. These promptings will tell us when and where we can be instruments in the Lord's hands so we can serve and love those around us. If time permits, tell the children about a time when you were prompted to serve and how it made you feel to be an instrument in the Lord's hands, or to do something that you know Jesus would have done if He were there.

Week 4: Heavenly Father Blesses Us through the Service We Give Each Other

SCRIPTURE

Alma 26:3

TALK

Theo's family lives in a place where there are sometimes big storms that rain very hard all over the area. Last year, one of those storms made a big mess in a city near Theo's house. Theo and his family were okay, but they knew that many other people were not. Lots of people had lost their houses, their food, and some of the other basic things they needed to survive. And there was lots of work to do, cleaning up the mess that the storm had made.

Theo and his family talked about how they could help. They gathered supplies and drove to the area where the storm had hit. When they got there, they worked hard. Theo helped by gathering up branches that had fallen from the trees. They put all the branches in a big pile so that other helpers could take them away. They also helped by clearing away mud and storm water and by passing out food and supplies to those who needed them.

The service that Theo and his family gave helped the people who had been in the storm, but it also helped Theo. He had a warm feeling inside that he knew was the Holy Ghost, telling him that Jesus and Heavenly Father were pleased with his service. Their family felt stronger because they had worked together to help. When we serve others, we bless them, and we are also blessed for serving. Service blesses everyone.

LESSON

DISCUSSION: Bring a group of five objects to show the children. It could be five pieces of fruit, five balls or toys, or five pieces of paper. Show the children the five objects. Then invite three children to the front and have them hold three of the objects. Ask the children how many you have left.

Explain that most of the time in our world, when we give something away, we are left with less. But that is not how it works when we are serving others. When we give something like our time or even our money to other people, Heavenly Father blesses us with more than we had before. In this way, service blesses the people that we serve, but it also blesses us.

ACTIVITY: Invite three children to come to the front of the room to act out the story of Elijah and the widow of Zarephath, as told in 1 Kings 17. You will need one girl to act as the widow, a boy to act as Elijah, and another boy to act as the widow's son. With younger children, you will likely want to be the narrator and tell the story in your own words. With older children, you could have the children who are watching read the chapter out loud while the children in front act out what is happening. You may want to dress the actors up in simple costumes.

APPLICATION AND REVIEW: Discuss how this scripture story illustrates the principle that when we serve others, they are blessed by our service and we are blessed for serving. Tell the children about a time when you felt blessed for service you gave. Testify that service is an important part of our Church, and it is important for each one of us because it brings us closer to Heavenly Father.

Chapter 10: October

I CAN SHARE THE GOSPEL

MULTIMEDIA RESOURCES

"6 Brothers," YouTube video, 3:44, posted by "Mormon Channel," January 10, 2012, www.youtube.com/watch?v=T0NRhsVDBXQ.

"The Value of a Full-time Mormon Mission," YouTube video, 5:22, posted by "Mormon Channel," July 3, 2012, www.youtube.com/watch?v=3aKU2rkvFQU&t=79s.

"Mormon Missionaries: An Introduction," YouTube video, 2:27, posted by "Mormon Channel," May 20, 2011, www.youtube.com/watch?v=YGnpHLS81lY.

"By Small and Simple Things: Sharing the Gospel," YouTube video, 3:15, posted by "LDS Youth," January 15, 2011, www.youtube.com/watch?v=HEoRCJ7MnJQ.

SONG LIST

- "I Want to Be a Missionary Now" (168)
- "I Hope They Call Me on a Mission" (169)
- "The Things I Do" (170)
- "We'll Bring the World His Truth" (172)

GOSPEL ART BOOK

Missionaries: Elders (no. 109)

Week 1: I Can Share the Gospel by Living It

SCRIPTURE

Matthew 5:16

TALK

Jesus taught His disciples that they should share the gospel with others. He told them that they should be a light for others to see. Being a light means sharing the happiness that the gospel brings to our lives. Light is a good symbol for the gospel because light helps people to see clearly, and the gospel can help us to see what is right and true.

We can let our lights shine by letting others see how the gospel makes us happy. This might mean inviting our friends to a fun Church activity. It could also mean talking to them about our family traditions, like studying the scriptures or saying family prayers. It definitely means being a good person and trying our best to choose the right. If we show others how much we love them and how much we love the gospel, they will learn to love the gospel too.

Jesus was a perfect example of being a light for others. He loved everyone, and He taught them the gospel because He knew it would make them happy. Not everyone listened to Him, but He let His light shine no matter what. We can follow Jesus's example and be a light for others each day.

LESSON

DISCUSSION: Ask an older child or teacher to recite the fourth Article of Faith. Have the children identify the first four principles and ordinances of the gospel. List them on the board.

1. Faith
2. Repentance
3. Baptism
4. The Holy Ghost

Explain that these principles form the foundation of our gospel and that as we live these principles, we will naturally find ways to share the gospel with others.
ACTIVITY: Divide the children into four groups, and assign each group one of the first four principles and ordinances. Have the children take a few minutes to create a skit that they can act out, showing how living this principle leads to sharing it. For example, the group assigned "baptism" might act out inviting friends and family to watch a child's baptism. Or the group assigned "repentance" might act out saying sorry to a friend after doing something hurtful.

Have the groups take turns presenting their skits to the other children. After all of the groups present, discuss with the children how living these gospel principles teaches others about our Church and what we believe.
APPLICATION AND REVIEW: Remind the children that they can be good missionaries now by not being afraid to live the gospel in a way that others can see. Share a few ways you have observed the children in your Primary living the gospel, and encourage them to continue doing so each day.

Week 2: I Can Share the Gospel by Being a Good Example

SCRIPTURE

1 Timothy 4:12

TALK

One time, Dominic was invited to go to the movies with a friend from school. At first, the movie seemed fun and silly, but as it kept going, Dominic felt uneasy. He knew that the movie was not something his parents would want him to watch. Dominic looked at his friend, but he seemed to be enjoying the movie. Dominic didn't know what to do.

Eventually, Dominic told his friend that he did not want to watch the rest of the movie. He said he would wait in the hall until the movie was over. To his surprise, Dominic's friend also wanted to leave. After they left, they decided to spend the rest of their time together playing games in the movie theater arcade. Dominic was glad they had left and so was his friend.

Sometimes, we can share the gospel with others by telling them about what we believe, but at other times, we can share the gospel simply by doing the right things. We can set a good example for our friends and family so that they will know that we really believe the things we say we believe. In this way, we can show our friends and family that we love being a part of our Church and that the gospel makes us happy.

LESSON

DISCUSSION: Tell the children that when Jesus lived on the earth, He set a perfect example for us in the way that He shared the gospel. At times, He shared the gospel by preaching to large or small groups of people. Other times, He shared the gospel simply by doing the right things. We sometimes say that He shared the gospel in the things that He said and in the way that He lived.

ACTIVITY: Have the children watch the video "I'm Trying to Be Like Jesus (Music Video)—Mormon Tabernacle Choir" that the "Mormon Tabernacle Choir" posted on YouTube (www.youtube.com/watch?v=oe2HZuEZG6I). As the children are watching, have them pay special attention to the ways that Jesus shared the gospel through His words and His actions.

APPLICATION AND REVIEW: When the video is over, ask the children to tell you some of the ways that Jesus shared the gospel. Each time they name a way, ask them how they could use that same way to share the gospel with their friends and family.

Bear your testimony of the importance of sharing the gospel with those around us. Testify that the gospel brings joy and light into our lives and that we can share this joy and light with others by being a good example. When we share the gospel with others, they will have the chance to feel the same happiness and peace that we do.

Week 3: My Family and Friends Need the Gospel

SCRIPTURE

D&C 88:81

TALK

Do you remember the story of Lehi's dream? Lehi dreamed that he was in a dark and dreary wilderness. He walked through it for what felt like hours. Finally, he became discouraged and cried out for help. Then he found himself in a big field. In the middle of the field was a beautiful tree, and this tree had fruit on it.

As soon as Lehi had tasted the fruit and knew for himself how good it was, the very next thing he wanted to do was share this good fruit with the rest of his family. He looked around to see if he could find them and when he saw them, he called to them to join him. Some members of Lehi's family, like his wife, Sariah, and his sons Nephi and Sam, came quickly and ate the fruit. But Lehi's other sons Laman and Lemuel would not come. This made Lehi sad.

In Lehi's dream, the fruit represents the gospel and the love of God. Lehi wanted to share these things with his family because they made him happy, and he wanted the people he loved to be happy too. It is natural to want to share the things that make us happy with the people we love. Our friends and family are special to us and we want them to be happy too. That's why we should share the gospel with them. Some of our friends and family members will want to know more about the gospel. Others may not want to know more right now. But it is important to keep sharing the gospel because the gospel will help our friends and family be happy in this life and forever.

LESSON

DISCUSSION: Explain to the children that the word "gospel" actually means "good news." Ask the children whom they usually like to tell when they have good news to share, or whom they want to talk to when something good happens to them. Discuss the fact that often we want to share our good news with the people we love most.

ACTIVITY: To illustrate how the good news of the gospel can spread when we share it with our family and friends, have all of the children sit down. Tap two children on the shoulder and say, "I want to share the gospel with you." Have the children who you shared the gospel with stand up. Then have these two children share the gospel with two more children. Repeat this until all of the children are standing. If time permits, you can repeat this activity, starting with two different children.

APPLICATION AND REVIEW: Ask the children to think of ways that they could naturally share the good news of the gospel with their friends and family. Make a list on the board, and encourage the children to choose one thing from the list that they could try this week. Tell the children that the gospel often spreads through small and simple things like an invitation to dinner, a thank-you note, or a kind action at school.

Week 4: My Testimony Grows When I Share It with Others

SCRIPTURE

D&C 65:2

TALK

Sierra's older brother is serving a mission. He spends a lot of his time sharing his testimony with other people. Sometimes the people he talks to want to know more about the gospel. Other times, they are not interested. But Sierra's brother says that he still loves to share his testimony because each time he talks about the things that he believes in, his own testimony grows a little more.

Sierra knows that this is true because she has felt the same thing. Sierra likes to share her testimony at family home evening, and sometimes she even speaks in fast and testimony meeting at church or gives talks in Primary. One time, she was able to talk with her friends at school about the Church. Whenever Sierra talks about the things that she believes, her testimony grows a little more.

This is true for all of us. It is not always easy to talk about the things that we believe in because these things are special to us. But we can follow the promptings of the Spirit that will tell us when we should share our testimonies. And each time we talk about the things that we believe in, our testimonies will grow a little more.

LESSON

DISCUSSION: Show the children a seed. Tell the children that Alma compared the word of God to a seed. He said that one way we could know whether the word of God was good was to plant this seed in our hearts and nourish it to see if it would grow. Just like we would plant a seed in the ground and take care of it to see if it grows into a plant. This is what we do when we try to help our testimonies grow. If there are parts of the gospel that we are not sure about, we can try to believe in them and see if they will grow in our hearts. Ask the children if they can think of some ways we might nourish the seeds of our faith or our testimonies.

Explain that one way we can nourish our testimonies is by sharing what we know with others. Even if we do not know everything about the gospel or we are not sure about some parts, we can share what we do know and the things we do believe in with others. This will help us to have more faith in them.

ACTIVITY: Invite one or two children to come to the front of the room and help you plant the seed that you showed the children at the beginning of the lesson. Explain that seeds need certain things to grow, like water, soil, and sunshine.

Ask the other children to think of specific ways or times that they could share their testimonies. Each time a child contributes an answer, give the seed a little more water to help it grow.

NOTE: If you would rather not plant an actual seed, or if you do not have the supplies necessary to do so, you can simply draw a seed on the board and add soil, raindrops, and sunshine to your picture as the children think of ways to share their testimonies.

APPLICATION AND REVIEW: Encourage the children to help their testimonies grow by sharing them with others. Bear your own testimony briefly and tell the children how thankful you are to be able to talk with them in Primary about the things that you know and believe.

Chapter 11: November

I CAN BE THANKFUL

MULTIMEDIA RESOURCES

"Daily Bread: Pattern," YouTube video, 2:51, posted by "Mormon Channel," September 6, 2013, www.youtube.com/watch?v=2eMJ6ZDCAp4.

"Thanksgiving Daily," YouTube video, 1:48, posted by "Mormon Channel," November 10, 2010, www.youtube.com/watch?v=wi0tqhedHIU.

"President Monson—'On Gratitude,'" YouTube video, 1:57, posted by "Mormon Channel," November 10, 2011, www.youtube.com/watch?v=W2f1kRWR6RM.

"#ThankfulFor," YouTube video, 2:12, posted by "Mormon Channel," November 24, 2014, www.youtube.com/watch?v=y_6KKDxz6u8.

SONG LIST

- "I Thank Thee, Dear Father" (7)
- "Children All Over the World" (16)
- "For Health and Strength" (21)
- "I Am Glad for Many Things" (151)

GOSPEL ART BOOK

Jesus Blesses the Nephite Children (no. 84)

Week 1: My Body Is a Sacred Gift from God

SCRIPTURE

D&C 88:15

TALK

In the summertime, Penelope loves to spend time at the pool. There are lots of different kids at the pool. Some of the kids are good at swimming, like Penelope. She likes to swim laps or race with other kids. But some of the kids are not as good at swimming. They just like to splash around or go down the waterslide. Sometimes Penelope likes to play with them too. The youngest kids at the pool, like Penelope's little brother, Jack, don't even know how to swim yet. All they can do is splash in the kiddie pool. And sometimes Penelope likes to do that too.

All of the kids look different too. Some kids are young, and some are older. Some kids are short, and some are taller. That is true for all people. We all look different. And we all have different talents and abilities. But one thing about us is the same: we have each been given a body from Heavenly Father.

He gave us bodies so we could learn how to take care of them. He wants us to use our bodies to do good things, like swimming, playing outside, and helping others.

Because our bodies come from Heavenly Father, they are sacred and special. We can show Heavenly Father that we are grateful for our bodies by taking good care of them. That includes being happy about the way we look, dressing modestly, staying clean and healthy, getting enough rest, and making sure that we only read, listen to, and watch good things.

LESSON

DISCUSSION: Tell the children that today you will be talking about a present. Have the children guess what this present might be. Give them a few clues or hints, such as, "This gift is something that we all have," and "We use this gift each day to do many different things." Explain that this special gift is our bodies. Our bodies are a gift from Heavenly Father, and they let us do all kinds of good things. We use our bodies to see, taste, smell, hear, and feel. We also use our bodies to work, play, and learn. Heavenly Father wants us to make good choices about the ways we use our bodies.

ACTIVITY: Invite a few children to come to the front of the room and take turns silently acting out some things they like to do with their bodies. If they have trouble thinking of an activity, ask them about their favorite sports or games. Have the other children guess what the children in front are doing.

APPLICATION AND REVIEW: Make sure the children know that their bodies are different, but that they are each special because they are gifts from Heavenly Father. He made us different and special because He knows that our differences can help us learn and grow. Ask the children to share some ways they plan to take care of their bodies this week. Then share something you plan to do to take care of your own body. Tell the children you are grateful for your body and all the things you can sense and enjoy because you have a body.

Week 2: Heavenly Father Blesses Me Daily

SCRIPTURE

Matthew 6:31–33

TALK

After the Israelites left Egypt, they had to travel in the wilderness for a long time. The Israelites were a large group of people, and there wasn't enough food in the wilderness for all of them. So Heavenly Father provided a miraculous way for them to get their food each day. He sent them food from heaven, and He gave them special instructions about what to do with it.

This food was called manna, and it appeared each morning. Heavenly Father told the Israelites to only gather enough manna to last them for one day. If they tried to keep it for longer than a day, it would go bad overnight, except on the day before the Sabbath. That day, they could gather enough for two days so that they could be prepared for the Sabbath, because the Sabbath was the only day when the manna did not appear. The Israelites stayed in the wilderness for a long time, and each day, Heavenly Father provided food for them to eat so they wouldn't be hungry.

Heavenly Father provides for us too. Though our food does not appear from the sky, Heavenly Father blesses us with so many things that we need every day. He has given us good food to eat, nice homes to live in, cars to help us get from place to place, fun places to play outside, good schools where we can learn, and so many other things that are all around us. Each day, we can pray to Heavenly Father to thank Him for giving us the daily blessings we see in our lives.

LESSON

DISCUSSION: Ask the children if they know what the word "physical" means. Explain that physical things are things we can see, smell, and touch. Tell the children that today you will be talking about physical blessings from Heavenly Father.

ACTIVITY: Play Gratitude Bingo. Have the children help you make a list of at least twenty temporal blessings from Heavenly Father that they are grateful for. Then give the children pieces of paper and have them fold their papers into sixteen sections by folding them in half four times. Have the children draw or write one blessing from the board in each section. You may need to help them write their blessings so that it does not take too long for them to prepare their boards.

When the children are ready, call out one blessing from the board and have the children mark that blessing on their papers if they have it. When a child gets four blessings in a row, that child wins the game. Keep going until a few children win, as time allows.

APPLICATION AND REVIEW: Tell the children that the only way to truly win at this gratitude game is to remember to thank Heavenly Father for all their blessings. Share a few physical blessings that you are especially grateful for, and encourage the children to thank Heavenly Father for their physical blessings in their prayers this week.

Week 3: Heavenly Father Blesses Me Spiritually

SCRIPTURE

1 Corinthians 2:9

TALK

A rich young man came to listen to Jesus teach. This young man had everything he wanted. He had a nice house and lots of fancy things. But Jesus told the young man that if he wanted to be truly righteous he needed to sell all of these things, give the money to the poor, and come follow Jesus. This made the young man sad.

This story of the young man teaches us that while it's nice to have riches and fancy things, these things are not the most important blessings we could have. If we are righteous, Heavenly Father will bless us with better riches than silver and gold or other treasures. Heavenly Father will bless us with spiritual gifts that will help us to return to Him.

These spiritual treasures include things like the scriptures, our families, and the lessons we learn through the Holy Ghost while we are at church or in the temple. In the scriptures, we can learn more about the spiritual gifts we can receive from Heavenly Father. Each of these gifts is very special, and we should try to use them to help other people. We should also remember to thank Heavenly Father for blessing us with these spiritual treasures in our lives because they will help us to return and live with Him again.

LESSON

DISCUSSION: Remind the children that last week you talked about physical blessings, which are the kinds of blessings we can see and touch in the world around us. But there is another kind of blessing that Heavenly Father gives us: spiritual blessings. Spiritual blessings include things like eternal families, the chance to repent, and the glorious kingdom we will live in with Heavenly Father after we die. They also include the spiritual gifts we have been given by Heavenly Father. Each of us has been given different spiritual gifts. The scriptures teach us about these gifts and tell us that we are to use them to help others, share the gospel, and build up the kingdom of God.

ACTIVITY: Using the chart below, write or tape the names from the third column ("person") on the board. Assign each class one of the spiritual gift verses from the first column. Have the classes read their verses and identify the spiritual gift described. Then have them take turns guessing which person on the board matches that spiritual gift. Point out that while some of the people on the board had many spiritual gifts and some of the spiritual gifts in this activity could have been given to more than one of the people listed, for the purposes of the activity, there is only one correct match.

When a class correctly guesses the person that had the spiritual gift they read about, have them read or summarize the scripture reference from the fourth column ("Demonstration of the Gift") for the entire Primary.

SPIRITUAL GIFT VERSE	SPIRITUAL GIFT	PERSON	DEMONSTRATION OF THE GIFT
D&C 46:13	Testimony of Christ	Abinadi	Mosiah 17:7–10
D&C 46:14	Belief on the testimony of others	Alma (the Elder)	Mosiah 17:1–2
D&C 46:19	Faith to be healed	The woman with the issue of blood	Mark 5:25–34
D&C 46:21	Working of miracles	Moses	Exodus 7:20; 8:12–13, 24, etc.
D&C 46:22	Prophecy	Isaiah	2 Nephi 2:11; 3 Nephi 23:1–3
D&C 46:25	Interpretation of tongues	Joseph Smith	Joseph Smith—History 1:62–67

APPLICATION AND REVIEW: Explain that there are additional spiritual gifts listed in the scriptures, including the faith to heal, speaking in tongues, the word of wisdom, and so forth. Help the children understand that some people are given different gifts than others and that this is part of Heavenly Father's plan. He made each one of us with different strengths and abilities. He wants us to work together and use all of our gifts to accomplish His work.

Week 4: I Am Thankful for All My Blessings

SCRIPTURE

D&C 59:7

TALK

As Jesus was traveling and teaching, He met ten men who were lepers. These men had a disease that made them unable to enter the city and live with their families. If they were not healed, they could die from this disease. The men asked Jesus to heal them.

Jesus told the men to go and show themselves to the priests, and as they went, they were healed. This was a miracle. The men were so excited to be healed, but only one of them turned back to thank Jesus for what He had done. When Jesus met this man, He asked him where the other nine men had gone. Then Jesus said that because this man had come to thank Him, Jesus would also forgive His sins. This man was healed on the inside and on the outside because he had been thankful.

When we are grateful, it can help us to feel better on the inside. Instead of thinking about all of the things we want and don't have, being grateful helps us think about the many wonderful things we do have. When we have gratitude in our hearts, we learn to be content and to thank Heavenly Father for our blessings, even if our lives are not perfect. This makes Heavenly Father happy. We should always remember to be grateful for the many blessings we have been given. This will help us to be happier, and it will help us to share our blessings with others so that they can be grateful too.

LESSON

DISCUSSION: Help the children understand that there may be times in their lives when it seems harder to be grateful for their blessings. When things are going wrong, we don't always feel like thanking Heavenly Father. But if we can stop and change our attitudes by thinking about the good things we have been given, we will be able to make better choices and we will feel closer to our Heavenly Father.

ACTIVITY: Bring a large piece of paper, like a poster, to Primary. Alternatively, you could bring several small pieces of paper that can be taped up together on the board to form a poster. In the middle of this poster or banner, write the words, "I Am Thankful for All My Blessings." Let the children decorate the rest of the paper with all of the things that they are thankful for. Encourage them to talk about the things that they are drawing with the children around them. At the end, display the poster on the board for the children to see. Point out a few drawings that you especially like and show the children how many things we've been blessed with.

APPLICATION AND REVIEW: Have the children choose something on the poster to thank Heavenly Father for in their prayers that night. Encourage them to keep a gratitude journal where they can continue to write down or draw pictures of the things that they are thankful for. Share with the children how being more grateful has helped you to recognize your blessings, make better choices, and grow closer to Heavenly Father.

Chapter 12: December

SOMEDAY JESUS WILL RETURN

MULTIMEDIA RESOURCES

"The Reason Behind Christmas," YouTube video, 3:43, posted by "Mormon Channel," January 28, 2014, www.youtube.com/watch?v=Urw4JUrul1Y.

"Chapter 19: The Second Coming of Jesus Christ," YouTube video, 3:02, posted by "Mormon Channel," May 14, 2012, www.youtube.com/watch?v=NNalljDgak4.

"He Lives: Testimonies of Jesus Christ," YouTube video, 2:09, posted by "Mormon Channel," March 29, 2010, www.youtube.com/watch?v=9ddXNF29goo&t=20s.

SONG LIST

- "Samuel Tells of the Baby Jesus" (36)
- "The Nativity Song (52)
- "When He Comes Again" (82)
- "Choose the Right Way" (160)

GOSPEL ART BOOK

The Second Coming (no. 66)

Week 1: Prophets Told of Baby Jesus

SCRIPTURE

1 Nephi 11:19–20

TALK

Isaiah was a prophet who lived long ago. He saw many visions of what would happen in the future, and he wrote down what he saw so that others would know what was coming. Isaiah saw that Jesus would be born as a baby on the earth. He saw many of the specific things that would happen when Jesus was born, and he wrote about them so that other people could look forward to the day when Jesus would arrive.

Nephi helped his people understand the prophecies of Isaiah so that they, too, could look forward to the day when Jesus would be born. The Nephites knew that Jesus would not visit them when He was born as a baby, but there were special signs of His birth that would tell the Nephites that Jesus had arrived. On the night when Jesus was born, there would be a day and a night and a day when the sun would go down, but the world would stay light.

When this happened, the Nephites knew that Jesus had finally been born. The righteous Nephites were so excited about Jesus's birth. The prophecies that had been written down by Isaiah and by their own prophets had finally come true! They knew that soon Jesus would come to visit them in their land after He had finished His ministry in Jerusalem.

LESSON

DISCUSSION: Tell the children that for hundreds of years, faithful people looked forward to the day when Jesus would be born. Many prophets were given visions of what would happen at His birth. Ask the children why the prophets and other people were so excited for Jesus to be born.

ACTIVITY: Write the song names from the following chart on pieces of paper. Then put these papers into a Christmas stocking or gift bag. Invite a child to come up and choose a paper from the stocking or bag. Sing the song, and then talk about the signs mentioned in the song that were foretold by ancient prophets. With older children, you may want to read the scripture verse that corresponds with each song.

SONG	SIGNS	SCRIPTURE VERSE
Samuel Tells of the Baby Jesus (36)	There would be a night that would be light like the day.	Helaman 14:3
Stars Were Gleaming (37)	Wise men or kings would follow a star to find Jesus.	Isaiah 60:3
When Joseph Went to Bethlehem (38)	Jesus would be born in Bethlehem.	Micah 5:2
Once within a Lowly Stable (41)	Jesus's mother would be named Mary.	Alma 7:10
The Nativity Song (52)	There would be a new star at His birth.	Helaman 14:5

APPLICATION AND REVIEW: Remind the children that at Christmastime the true reason for our celebrations is to remember the Savior. Testify that the prophets knew of Jesus's birth long before it happened. They looked forward to His coming because they knew that He would atone for their sins and conquer death. Encourage the children to think about ways that they could honor the Savior this Christmas season. Share one way you are going to try to remember Jesus as you celebrate Christmas this year.

Week 2: Someday Jesus Will Come Again

SCRIPTURE

D&C 45:44–45

TALK

Sometimes Sammie used to see scary things on the news when she watched TV with her dad. When Sammie's parents realized that watching the news was making her afraid and worried, they told her they needed to talk. Sammie's parents explained that many of the sad or scary things she had noticed were signs that were foretold in the scriptures. A long time ago, prophets were shown the kinds of things that would happen in our day. They wrote about these things so that we would know that when we saw them, something good would be coming soon. That good thing is Jesus's Second Coming, when He will return to the earth. Even though Sammie was excited about Jesus returning, she was still a little nervous about all of these signs, until her parents explained that if we make good choices and are prepared, we do not need to be afraid.

The scriptures tell us that if we are righteous, we will be protected when Jesus comes again. That means that we can look forward to His return without fear. Now Sammie knows that she doesn't need to worry.

Our world can seem like it is full of scary things, but these are actually signs that Jesus will return again. And it is important to remember that there are more good things happening than what you see on the news. The world is also filled with kind, happy people who are looking forward to Jesus's return. We can look forward to it also and prepare ourselves now for that happy day that will come in the future.

LESSON

DISCUSSION: Tell the children that you are thinking about a special event that will happen in the future. Ask them to raise their hands to guess what the event is. Give them some clues, such as, "This event will change the lives of everyone on earth," and "Many prophets have seen this event in visions." When one of the children has correctly guessed that the event is Jesus's Second Coming, ask the children what they know about the Second Coming.

ACTIVITY: Display the pictures from the chart below around the Primary room. (Each picture can be found in the *Gospel Art Book*.) Invite the children to help you sort the pictures into two columns on the board, depending on whether the picture is related to Jesus's birth or His Second Coming.

JESUS'S BIRTH	JESUS'S SECOND COMING
Joseph and Mary Travel to Bethlehem (no. 29)	The Ascension of Jesus (no. 62)
The Birth of Jesus (no. 30)	The Second Coming (no. 66)
The Angel Appears to the Shepherds (no. 31)	Christ and Children from around the World (no. 116)

When you have correctly sorted the pictures, have the children observe some things that might be different about the two events. For instance, you could point out that when Jesus was born as a baby, only a few people were able to witness the event. But when Jesus returns, His Second Coming will be glorious, and many people will know that He is here.

APPLICATION AND REVIEW: To conclude your discussion, sing the song, "When He Comes Again," (82). Encourage the children to look forward with faith to Jesus's Second Coming and do all they can to prepare for that exciting and sacred event. Bear your testimony that someday Jesus will return to the earth with power and glory to reign in righteousness.

Week 3: I Can Live with Jesus and Heavenly Father Again

SCRIPTURE

D&C 33:17

TALK

Last year, something sad happened in Arthur's family. His grandpa got sick and, a few months later, he died. Arthur was sad to lose his grandpa. He misses the time they spent together: going to baseball games, going on vacations, and working outside in the yard. But Arthur knows that someday he will see his grandpa again.

Heavenly Father's plan of salvation makes it possible for all of us to live again after we die. Someday, Arthur and his grandpa will be resurrected and receive bodies again. These bodies will be perfect, celestial bodies that we can keep forever. Arthur and his grandpa will also have the chance to live with Jesus and Heavenly Father again.

The choices we make in our lives now will determine whether or not we can return and be with Heavenly Father. Arthur knows that Heavenly Father loves him even more than his grandpa does. Both Heavenly Father and Arthur's grandpa would want him to try to always choose the right. When it is time for Arthur to be resurrected, he can live with his grandpa and Heavenly Father forever. Each day, Arthur tries to do the right things so that someday he can be reunited with his grandpa and Heavenly Father.

LESSON

DISCUSSION: Ask the children what they have done to prepare for Christmas this year. With younger children, you may need to explain that the word "prepare" means "to get ready." It is fun to prepare for Christmas by decorating our houses and wrapping presents. Tell the children that there is another wonderful thing that they can prepare for each day. They can prepare to return to Heavenly Father and live with Him forever. Ask the children what things they could do to prepare to return to Heavenly Father and live with Him.

ACTIVITY: Display the picture Parable of the Ten Virgins (no. 53) from the *Gospel Art Book*. With older children, have them take turns reading verses from Matthew 25:1–13. With younger children, summarize this parable in your own words. Depending on the size of your Primary, you could invite several children to come up and act out the parable while the other children read the scripture verses. Discuss what this parable teaches us about being prepared. Explain that while this parable is meant to help us prepare for Jesus's Second Coming, it is also applicable to preparing to live with Heavenly Father and Jesus again after we die.

APPLICATION AND REVIEW: Emphasize the idea that we cannot simply prepare at the last minute. We must make good choices throughout our lives so that we are ready to live with Heavenly Father again and feel comfortable in His presence. We must learn how to repent when we make mistakes and try harder to be better. Encourage the children to form good gospel habits now, when they are young, so that they can keep these habits strong throughout their lives.

Week 4: I Know I Am a Child of Heavenly Father

SCRIPTURE

Moses 1:13

TALK

One time, Moses was praying on a high mountain. Heavenly Father appeared to Moses, and they talked together. Later, Satan appeared and tried to make Moses worship him. Satan could not trick Moses because Moses knew that he was a son of God. Moses knew the difference between God and Satan. He knew Heavenly Father was more powerful than Satan, and Moses knew that Heavenly Father loved him.

Moses told Satan to leave, but Satan would not go. So Moses prayed for help. Moses used the power of God to make Satan leave. After Satan was gone, Moses saw God again. Heavenly Father showed Moses a vision of all the people who would ever live on the earth.

All of the people on earth are children of God. Like Moses, each one of us can know that we are Heavenly Father's children. We may not see God and Satan like Moses did, but each of us can pray and gain a testimony that we are children of God. This testimony helps us know the difference between Heavenly Father and Satan so that Satan will not be able to trick us with his lies. When you know that you are a child of God and that He loves you, you have the power to know what is true, to make good choices, and to follow Heavenly Father's plan so that someday you can return to Him.

LESSON

DISCUSSION: Ask the children to think about a time when they were lost. Ask them how it felt when they did not know which way to go. Explain that many people around us feel lost because they do not know who they are or where they are going. They do not know that they are children of God and that they lived with Heavenly Father before they were born. Tell the children that knowing we are children of God gives us power to help people who feel lost. We can help them feel Heavenly Father's love for them.

ACTIVITY: Have the children watch the video, "I Am a Child of God" posted by "Mormon Channel" on YouTube (www.youtube.com/watch?v=JOrcqqpHCt8), and instruct them to listen to the words of the song. Ask them to listen for specific blessings that Heavenly Father has given us. When the song is over, call on a few children to share the blessings they heard in the song. Then ask the children if they know of any other blessings our Heavenly Father has given us.

APPLICATION AND REVIEW: Remind the children that when they have a strong testimony of their divine nature and potential as children of God, they will have power to overcome Satan. They will know that their blessings come from a loving Father in Heaven, and they will be able to share this knowledge with others and develop a deeper relationship with Heavenly Father and Jesus Christ.

Primary Presentation

The annual primary sacrament meeting presentation is an opportunity for the children in Primary to share what they have been learning with the rest of the ward or branch. Elaborate visuals, costumes, or videos are not appropriate for sacrament meeting. Focus instead on bringing the Spirit with music and simple testimonies. Try to keep your expectations age-appropriate. Younger children may only be able to memorize a short line. On the other hand, you can keep older children engaged by asking them to perform some of the songs in small groups or to give longer talks. Organizing the children by their classes can help them to know when it will be their turn to speak.

This chapter begins with some general tips and ideas for preparing and giving your presentation. After this section, you'll find a sample outline for the presentation that you can adapt to the needs of your children.

LEARNING THE SONGS FOR YOUR PRESENTATION

Music is a key part of your presentation and can help each child participate more actively. Help the children learn these six suggested songs by practicing them in different ways throughout the year.

"I Am a Child of God" (2)

Most of the children will already know this song, but they may not understand the profound doctrines behind the words they are singing. Be sure to discuss these with them or ask them to tell you, in their own words, what the lyrics mean. You can come back to this song several times throughout the year whenever you talk about strengthening your relationship with Heavenly Father. Encourage the younger children to memorize the first verse of the song and try to have the older children memorize all of the verses.

You can also use this song as an opportunity to teach dynamics and musical phrasing to the older children. Tell them which word you think is most important in each line and teach them how to stress that word slightly as they sing. When leading the music, move your arms out and then back in to show when the children should sing louder or softer.

"My Heavenly Father Loves Me" (228)

The lyrics in this song are filled with beautiful descriptions and images. You can help the children remember the words by having them draw simple pictures to illustrate each line, as outlined in the chart below. When you sing this song, invite several children to come to the front of the room and hold these illustrations up in order. Point to each picture as you sing the line it illustrates.

VERSE 1

LYRICS	ILLUSTRATION
Whenever I hear the song of a bird	A bird
Or look at the blue, blue sky,	A blue sky
Whenever I feel the rain on my face	Raindrops
Or the wind as it rushes by,	Swirls to indicate the wind blowing
Whenever I touch a velvet rose	A rose
Or walk by our lilac tree,	A lilac tree, or simply a tree
I'm glad that I live in this beautiful world	The earth
Heav'nly Father created for me.	A child

VERSE 2

LYRICS	ILLUSTRATION
He gave me my eyes that I might see	Eyes
The color of butterfly wings.	A colorful butterfly
He gave me my ears that I might hear	Ears
The magical sound of things.	Sparkles or stars to indicate magic
He gave me my life, my mind, my heart:	A heart
I thank him rev'rently	A child praying
For all his creations, of which I'm a part.	The sun, moon, and stars
Yes, I know Heav'nly Father loves me.	Heavenly Father

"If the Savior Stood Beside Me" (available online at LDS.org or in the October 1993 edition of the *Friend* magazine)

When you first begin learning this song, read the words aloud to the children. Explain that the first two verses are full of questions. The first verse asks questions about our actions, and the second verse asks questions about our words. Then the third verse explains that even though we cannot see the Savior standing next to us, He is always close by and He sees and blesses us for our efforts to choose the right.

After you have discussed the words, let the children listen to the melody without trying to sing along. Teach them one line at a time, taking care to point out where the emphasis of each line should be placed. Note that the timing in this song can be a little tricky for children to follow, so you may want to sing the line to them and then have them sing it back to you. Continue in this way until you have learned all the lines in the first verse. Then sing the whole verse together. Repeat this method until you have learned all three verses. While it may seem painstaking to learn only one line at a time, keep in mind that this song may be new or unfamiliar to many of the children. Be sure to plan enough time to help them learn the words and what those words mean.

"When I Am Baptized" (103)

Help the children memorize this song by teaching them hand motions to go along with the lyrics. Use the chart below as a guide, or make up your own motions. As the children learn, you can invite one or two children to come to the front of the room to perform the motions and guide the other children.

VERSE 1

KEYWORD	HAND MOTIONS
Rainbows	Move right hand in an arc from left to right
Rain	Move hands down with fingers wiggling
Earth	Move both hands down in a circular motion, beginning with hands together, then moving out, then meeting together again

CHORUS

KEYWORD	HAND MOTIONS
My life	Place one hand on chest or heart
Earth	Move both hands down in a circular motion, beginning with hands together, then moving out, then meeting together again
Rain	Move hands down with fingers wiggling
Best I Can	Swing right arm up and to the left with fist clenched
God	Raise right hand slightly with palm facing up and look up toward heaven

VERSE 2

KEYWORD	HAND MOTIONS
Washed Away	With palms facing down, move both hands in and out a few times
Forgiven	Cross arms over chest
Improve	With palm facing down, raise right hand to indicate going from a lower level to a higher level

"Families Can Be Together Forever" (188)

We sing this Primary song often, so many of the children will already know it. To check that they have learned it correctly, bring a small beanbag or plush toy to Primary. As you are singing, have the children watch you closely. Pause the music at random intervals and then gently toss the beanbag or toy to one child. Have the child sing or say the next word in the song. This child could then pass the beanbag or toy back to you and you could direct the music to begin again so you can continue singing. Or you could have the child toss the beanbag or toy to another child, who then has to sing or say the next word in the song. If the children are not sure about what comes next, sing the song all together again to review it.

The 4/4 timing of this song makes it a good one to teach the children basic conducting skills. Have them follow along with your arm movements as you conduct the singing. Then invite one or more children to come to the front of the room and conduct the others as you sing the song again.

"A Child's Prayer" (12)

This is another song that will be familiar to many of the older children. With younger children, focus on learning the two parts separately. Make sure the children know the parts well before you try to sing them together.

To add variety to your practices with the older children, you can assign different groups to sing the different parts. For example, you could have the girls sing one part and the boys sing the other. You could have the children sing one part while the teachers sing the other. Or you could have children whose birthdays fall in the first part of the year sing the first part and the children whose birthdays fall in the second part of the year sing the second part. Write down several possible ways to break up the groups on slips of paper. Then put these papers in a bag and have one child come up and choose how to divide into groups. Remember that the more you sing this song, the better the children will learn it.

PREPARING FOR YOUR PRESENTATION

In addition to having the children practice the songs and their individual speaking parts, you will want to have them practice reverence on the stand, how to conduct themselves during the meeting, and how to speak into the microphone correctly. To this end, you may want to plan to have the Primary give a special musical number in sacrament meeting in August or even July. This will give you a chance to teach the children how to reverently walk to the front of the chapel, assemble themselves to sing, and project their voices. You could also try introducing a microphone in sharing time and having the children who participate in the lesson that day try using the microphone to answer questions or read scriptures. You may want to come up with a simple hand symbol for reverence that you use in your Primary. Make sure the children know what it is and what it means so that you can use it to signal to them nonverbally during the Primary presentation and during your practices.

Practices for the presentation should not take away unnecessarily from family time. If you have a large Primary, you might consider breaking your practices into sessions for junior and senior Primary. You might also think about providing coloring pages or some other quiet activity for younger children to keep them occupied while the older ones are practicing their parts. In general, it is best to practice special musical numbers, like those performed by only one child or one class, separately, so as not to waste time with the larger group.

If you plan to have the children sit on the stand for the entire meeting, you will want to plan a seating arrangement that ensures reverence. If necessary, separate children who cannot sit next to each other without distracting others. Be strategic in where you place teachers.

Have the children practice standing and making their way to the microphone reverently. If possible, give the children their parts as early as you can so that they have time to learn them before the presentation. Don't worry about perfection as you're practicing, and avoid stopping your practice to fix little things. The point is to help the children get used to the overall flow of the presentation.

SAMPLE PRESENTATION IDEAS

It's a good idea to begin the presentation with a short introduction from a member of the Primary presidency. You could say,

> This year in Primary we have been learning about our relationship with Heavenly Father. We have learned that we are children of a loving Father in Heaven. Each of us has come to earth to gain a body and join a family as part of our Father's great plan of happiness. We have learned that while we are here, we can choose to follow the examples set by Jesus and by the prophets. We have learned that the true gospel was restored, and that we can be baptized into Jesus's Church, keep the commandments, and repent when we make mistakes. We can pray to our Heavenly Father and He will hear us and answer our prayers. We have learned that we can share the gospel with our friends and family by loving and serving them. We are grateful for Heavenly Father's plan. As we continue to learn and grow, we want to strengthen our relationship with our Heavenly Father so that someday we can return to live with Him again.

You may want to have an older child or group of older children act as narrators throughout the presentation, introducing each new monthly topic. Alternatively, you could ask one of the teachers or leaders to fill this role. The remainder of this sample outline will follow the structure below:

Topic: Simple introduction that could be given by a teacher or narrator.

- Sample line for young children
- Sample part for older children
- Idea for a talk from one older child

You do not need to include both older and younger children for each topic. Use the Spirit to help you create a structure and presentation that works for the children in your Primary. Try to leave time at the end of your presentation for a member of the bishopric to offer some brief remarks.

SAMPLE OUTLINE

Introduction from Primary presidency (see above).

Song: "I Am a Child of God"

God Is Our Father: All of us are children of God. We lived with Him before we were born. He knows and loves each one of us. He has sent us here to help us learn to make good choices, so that someday we can return and live with Him again.

- I know that I am a child of God. He loves me.
- Heavenly Father has a plan for my life. Before I was born, I chose to follow this plan. Now that I am here on earth, I can continue to make good choices and follow Heavenly Father's plan. I know that His plan will help me to be happy forever.
- You could have one of the older children give an overview of the plan of salvation or talk about the Council in Heaven. Have the child testify that we are all children of God, that He knows and loves each one of us individually, and that His plan is designed to lead us back to Him, so that we can live with Him eternally.

The Creation: Jesus and Heavenly Father created the earth for us because They knew we would need a place where we could gain a body and learn to choose between right and wrong. This beautiful earth is a gift from our Heavenly Father.

- Jesus Christ created the earth for us under the direction of Heavenly Father.
- Our world is full of opposites. These opposites help us know the difference between right and wrong. Adam and Eve chose to leave the Garden of Eden and experience these opposites so that we could all learn how to choose the right.
- You could have an older child outline the different days or time periods that made up the Creation. The child could also share some of their favorite creations or things in nature. Have the child express gratitude for the beautiful world Heavenly Father made for us.

Song: "My Heavenly Father Loves Me"

The Savior: Jesus Christ suffered for our sins so that we would not have to suffer if we would repent. He died and was resurrected to conquer death. Because Jesus was resurrected, we will all live again after we die.

- Jesus loves me so much that He died for me. He atoned for us because He loves us.
- We refer to Jesus as our Savior because He has saved us from death and eternal punishment. When we repent, we can access His atoning power, which means that we do not have to suffer for our sins because He has already suffered for them.

- You could have an older child recite the third article of faith and explain what it means to be obedient to the laws and ordinances of the gospel. You could also have this child share an experience when they made a mistake and needed to repent. Then have the child testify of the power of Christ's atoning sacrifice.

Song: "If the Savior Stood Beside Me"

The Restoration: After Jesus died, His true Church and power were lost from the earth for a long time. Joseph Smith restored this true Church and the priesthood power that blesses our lives through covenants and ordinances.

- In our Church, we have the priesthood, which is the power of God.
- When Joseph Smith prayed to know which church to join, Heavenly Father and Jesus Christ appeared to him and told him that the true Church was no longer on the earth. Joseph soon learned that he would need to restore the true Church of Christ in our day.
- An older child could tell the story of the First Vision in their own words. Then the child could share a brief testimony of the prophet Joseph Smith and the restored gospel.

Prophets: God's Church has always been led by prophets. We are blessed to have a living prophet on the earth, who can receive revelation and tell us the things that Jesus wants us to know today.

- Jesus is the head of our Church. He directs our prophet, and the prophet tells us what Jesus wants us to know.
- Our prophet sets an example for us and teaches us what we need to know in our day. I am learning how to follow the prophet. I know that when I follow His example and am obedient to His counsel, I will be blessed.
- You could have an older child talk about their favorite talk from general conference or share one way that they are trying to follow the prophet's counsel. Have the child share a brief testimony of the living prophet.

Song: "When I Am Baptized"

Baptism: Each of us can follow Jesus's example by being baptized by immersion. When we are baptized, we become members of His Church and are blessed with the gift of the Holy Ghost. The Holy Ghost comforts us and guides us. He also testifies of truth.

- Someday I want to be baptized. I can prepare now to be baptized when I am eight.

- My baptism day was a special day. All of my sins were washed away, and I was clean and pure. Now that I am baptized, I can renew my covenants by partaking of the sacrament each week.
- You could have an older child give a brief talk on the gift of the Holy Ghost and how this gift has made a difference in the child's life. Have the child discuss the different roles the Holy Ghost plays in our lives, such as being a comforter, a testifier of truth, and a voice of warning when we are in danger.

Families: We are grateful for the blessing of being part of a family. We know that because of Heavenly Father's plan, we can live with our families forever. We want to help our families be happy here and in the eternities.

- I love my family so much. I'm glad Heavenly Father sent me to live in my family.
- My parents have taught me how to live the gospel by their actions and by their words. I am grateful that my father holds the priesthood and can use it to bless our family. I know that our family can be together forever because my parents have been sealed in the temple.
- Have an older child discuss "The Family: A Proclamation to the World" and the lessons that it teaches us about how families are central to Heavenly Father's plan. Have the child talk about what makes a family successful. Have them share some ways that the child is trying to strengthen their family.

Song: "Families Can Be Together Forever"

Prayer: When we pray, we can communicate with our Heavenly Father through Jesus Christ. Prayer is a special opportunity for us to thank Heavenly Father for the blessings He has given us and ask for the things that we need.

- Heavenly Father hears and answers my prayers, and He hears and answers yours too.
- Heavenly Father doesn't always answer my prayers in the way that I think He will. Sometimes I don't recognize the answers He sends until later, but I know that He always answers my prayers in the way that is best for me because He loves me.
- An older child could share a scripture story that teaches us about prayer, such as the story of Enos in the Book of Mormon. Have the child tell the story in their own words and then discuss the lessons this story teaches us about how to pray or how Heavenly Father answers prayers.

Song: "A Child's Prayer"

Service: We know that when we serve the people around us, we are really serving our Heavenly Father. He blesses us with opportunities to serve and help our neighbors. We want to follow the example Jesus set and show charity and love to all.

- I can serve the people around me by being kind.
- There are many people we can serve. I try to serve the members of my family, my friends at school, the people in my neighborhood, and the people I see at church each week. Jesus taught us to love one another and to serve our neighbors, which means all of the people around us.
- Have an older child discuss a service project that they organized or participated in. Ask the child to share how serving others made him or her feel, and how this service has prepared the child to continue to serve in the future.

Missionary Work: We are so excited to share the gospel with our friends and family! We know that we can share the gospel by being good examples, and that our testimonies grow when we share them.

- One way that I can share the gospel is by living it and letting my light shine.
- I know that my friends and family will learn about the gospel by the example I set. If I am kind and loving, they will know that the gospel teaches us how to love others. I can share the gospel just by being a good example.
- You could ask an older child to talk about a missionary experience they had. The child could also talk about how they are preparing to serve a full-time mission someday, and why they are looking forward to that opportunity to serve the Lord.

Song: "I Want to Be a Missionary Now," "The Things I Do," or another song of your choice

Gratitude: Heavenly Father has blessed us with so many things. Some of our blessings are physical and others are spiritual. We are learning to thank Him for all our blessings. Being grateful helps us to be happy and content.

- I am grateful for my home and family and for the things I learn in Primary.
- Heavenly Father has blessed me with a special temple called a body. I can show Heavenly Father that I am grateful for my body by eating healthy foods and being careful about what I watch, listen to, and read.

- Have an older child discuss the spiritual gifts that Heavenly Father has given us. Have them share a few examples from the scriptures or from people in their own life who were blessed with specific spiritual gifts.

The Second Coming: Jesus was born as a baby in Jerusalem. He lived a perfect life. Someday, He will return to the earth in great power and glory. We are looking forward to the day when Jesus will come again.

- I know Jesus will return someday. I can prepare for His coming by living righteously.
- The tenth article of faith tells us that Christ will return and "reign personally upon the earth." I know that when Jesus comes again, many people will be blessed. I want to choose the right so I can live with Heavenly Father and Jesus again.
- You could ask an older child to discuss their feelings about the Second Coming. Have the child talk about some ways that they are trying to live the gospel and prepare to return to Heavenly Father. Ask the child to conclude by testifying that we are all children of God.

Song: "When He Comes Again" or another song of your choice

Closing remarks from a member of the bishopric.

About the Author

HEIDI DOXEY is the author of seven previous volumes in the Tiny Talks and Time to Share series, one novel, and two board books: *1, 2, 3 with Nephi and Me!* and *Jesus Was Just like Me.*

Heidi blogs at girlwithalltheanswers.blogspot.com. She currently lives in a tiny house in the San Francisco Bay Area, and works as an assessment developer for Western Governors University. In addition to writing, Heidi enjoys going to the beach, playing volleyball, and traveling to visit her family and friends.

Scan to visit

www.girlwithalltheanswers.blogspot.com